Thanks for the insight on this most inspiring section of God's Word [see chapter 1]. You truly are the master teacher and I keep learning from you! — RL, San Diego CA

Thank you, Peter. What a beautiful, encouraging word, to read the word as a love letter from our Dear Lord! [see chapter 5]. I will be sharing this with my friends. — Joan, internet

Peter, my Bible got stolen when I had packed up everything in my truck, as I was heading out on a 1000-mile relocation the next day. I was so lost! I had marked in it whatever I could so it was quite "colorful." It took me two straight weeks to re-mark my new Cambridge bible. [see chapter 6] — BO, Charleston WV

Andrew Farley's quote about a belief system that results in a "slower death," a mix lacking the stringency of the Old Testament Law or the full enjoyment of New Testament Grace [see chapter 5] also describes what I once thought to be the "balanced" walk of a Christian believer. You remind me (over and over again!) how unfruitful and impossible it is to try and mix this "law and grace" thinking together. The two simply cannot go hand-in-hand. Thank you for this sharing! Acts 29! I love it! [see chapter 7] — SR, Lexington KY

"Great grace" is great! [see chapter 11] — GV, Oak Harbor WA

Because many Christians have found the Bible to be too difficult to understand, they have turned to Christian books relating personal experiences as their main meal. I think this teaching would be helpful and might woo them back to the Bible [see chapter 13]. — IB, Walnut Creek CA.

Wow...thanks!!! concerning all that you wrote here [see chapter 14]... — Anna, internet

Sure like what you wrote. That has perfect LIFE and PEACE in it and BLESSINGS your way and keep speaking the TRUTH!! [see chapter 15] — JH, Huntingdon IN

Also by Peter Wade:

Enjoy Your Bible...
and understand it too!

Peter Wade

POSITIVE
WORD
MINISTRIES

Some chapters are adapted from other works by the author, and some first appeared in his email newsletter. Website addresses are correct at the time of publication.

* * *

My thanks to:
Vivien Wade, who has shared in my ministry for 60 years; Irene Baroni for her great editorial services; and supporters of this ministry, both in Australia and the United States, who have made this book possible.

https://www.PeterWade.com

Positive Word Ministries Inc., 39 Schooner Road, Seaford SA 5169, Australia
Positive Words Inc., 15119 Barbee Ct, San Jose CA 95127-1201, USA.
Version 2.2
The first edition is available as a Kindle eBook

Contents

First Words

In this book I hope to motivate and inspire you to read your Bible. I want you to see the simplicity of how the Bible can teach you, and how you can enjoy it.

Certainly there are parts of the Bible that are harder to understand, as we see from Jesus' statement in John 16:25, *"These things have I spoken unto you in proverbs: but the time cometh, when I shall no more speak unto you in proverbs, but I shall shew you plainly of the Father"* (KJV). I have included an Appendix to further illustrate this and similar verses. Peter told us in II Peter 3:16 about Paul's letters, *"There are some things in them that are hard to understand..."*

Yet the majority of the English Bible can be understood even by those whose second language is English. In one of the first books I purchased in my late teens (see chapter 5), the author stated, "In the mastery of the Bible there are two great principles, both of supreme importance. Here they are: First: Treat the Bible as you treat any other book. Second: Treat the Bible as you treat no other book. In other words. treat the Bible, first, **naturally**, and then, **spiritually**." And naturally is where we must start.

The Bible was not written to be a repository of quotations, like the book of Proverbs. Most of the 66 books contained in what we call the Holy Bible were written to be read like any other book, that is, from the first word consecutively to the last word. Yet on television most of the preachers will take a verse from here and one from there, without regard for the context. That is not the natural way of reading a book, and the same is true of the Bible.

First, to understand the Bible you need an enquiring mind, hungry to learn. The fictional character Sherlock Holmes said, "The world is full of obvious things which nobody ever observes." This is also true of the Bible.

Second, you need an essentially literal translation of the Bible, like the King James Version (KJV), the New King James Version (NKJV), the New American Standard Bible (NASB), the English Standard Version (ESV; used primarily in this book) and others. There are many versions that are a paraphrase of the Bible text, bringing out what the translator thought the writer would have written if it were today, known as dynamic equivalent versions. These include the New Living Translation, the Message, the New International Version, and the Mirror Bible. (I will discuss translations versus paraphrases in chapter 16.)

Finally, you need a Bible you are not afraid to write on. I do not believe in bibliolatry, that is worshipping the copy of the book itself, as with the Quran (Islam). Yet I do hold the Word of God in great respect, and there is no disrespect in marking the Bible as you would any other study book. (I will discuss marking your Bible in chapter 6.)

Okay, on to the first chapter and an illustration using the most beloved chapter of the Bible, Psalm 23.

1
The Lord is My Shepherd

One vital part of the teaching program of most churches is missing: that of teaching believers how to **enjoy** their Bible. Most seem content to have followers in the Sunday service as spectators to a show plus some points to help them in the coming week, and don't forget to come next Sunday! I want to demonstrate how easy it is to get daily encouragement from reading your own Bible.

Possibly the most well-known and constantly used passage is Psalm 23, written by David. It is almost universally used at funerals, the hymn versions are also favorites, and I would guess a majority of church attendees could recite it from memory. It is really best discussed at Easter, as it follows Psalm 22, the psalm of the Cross. Let's use it to show how to enjoy your Bible without a college degree!

My first suggestion is this: **simply read what is written!**

"The Lord is my shepherd" (Psalm 23:1a ESV). It is interesting that most of the popular translations and para-phrases do not attempt to change the words of this phrase from the original 1611 edition of the King James Version. I suspect this is because the phrase is so ingrained in English speech and literature. There are no long words here; just five

simple words that just about everyone understands.

Notice first that the statement is about a *relationship* between "The Lord" and "me," that is you! And this relationship continues through the six verses of the psalm. "He makes me...," "he leads me...," "he restores my...," and so on. Underline the me's, the my's, the I's. Put a circle around "The Lord," the he's, the thy's, the thou's (or you's and your's, depending on your translation).

Let us not pass over the *present* tense "is" in this phrase. (The verb tenses indicate time.) I just read an autobiography that spoke of the writer's parents having "a profound faith in an ever-present God." "Is" speaks of just that. Christianity that is not present tense is the greatest curse this world has known. Today, as you read this, "The Lord IS my shepherd." It is not only present tense, it is *personal* — "MY shepherd." He is a shepherd to me! Say it over and over again. "The Lord is MY shepherd." Right at this moment it is true, and right through this day and night it remains true. If you tread on an ant or kick the cat, it is still true! There is no "if" nor "but" nor even "I hope so." "The Lord IS MY shepherd."

Now let us think for a moment about to whom this phrase refers. Since it is in the Old Testament, "The Lord" is not the Lord Jesus Christ but "the God and Father of our Lord Jesus Christ" (Ephesians 1:3). Perhaps the notes in your Bible might tell you the word translated is "Jehovah-Ro'i," one of the compound names of God in the Old Testament. However, even without understanding the distinction we can still get a bucket of truth from this one phrase.

At the end of the phrase in the English translation we have the word "shepherd." Surely everyone knows a shepherd is a person who looks after sheep, so God is looking after me. A shepherd takes his sheep where there is food and water. He

PETER WADE

protects them from predators. He knows each one by name.
He sleeps with them at night, after counting them to check they
are all gathered together. That is how God is looking after me
right now.

The first verse in its completeness reads *"The Lord is my
shepherd; I shall not want"* or "I shall not lack" (AMP). The
reason I shall not lack is because "The Lord is my shepherd."
I might lack otherwise, but I won't now because the Lord is
my shepherd, for he supplies all my need.

So verse 1 is *present tense,* it is *personal,* and it details
God's *provision.* The rest of the Psalm describes how he looks
after us and gives examples of circumstances in which we
should remember this.

Read the Psalm 23 in your favorite translation or
paraphrase right now, and then give Him thanks for His love
and care for you.

A New Testament example of this great relationship
between God and you can be found in Paul's letter to the
Ephesians. *"Even as he chose us in him before the foundation
of the world, that we should be holy and blameless before
him"* (Ephesians 1:4). Let's look at the personal pronouns: He,
us, and him. *"Even as he [God] chose us [the saints, the
faithful (verse 1)] in him [Christ Jesus]."* Who said that Bible
study is difficult and dull?

There is tremendous truth in those three little words: **He,
us and him**; in fact, the whole scope of theology. I'm blessed
to learn that I am associated with God and Christ Jesus, and
I'm in the middle! It's He, us and him, and that's a winning
combination! We have a connection that this world does not
comprehend. And we we can just read what God has written,
without the need of a considerable study.

10

2
The Joy and Rejoicing of my Heart

To many people, the Bible is an old-fashioned book that's fine for little old ladies and funerals but of limited or no value in their daily lives. How wrong they are! To me, the Bible is an exciting book and more up-to-date than tomorrow's newspaper.

I want to explore with you this verse from Jeremiah 15:16, "*Your words were found, and I ate them, and your words became to me a joy and the delight of my heart.*" So we can enjoy the Bible as a book that delights us; for if one person has found God's words enjoyable, then all people can. "They were as welcome to him as food is to a hungry man; he cheerfully received them, treasured them up in his memory, digested them in his mind, and carefully retained them" (John Gill)."

E.W. Bullinger in the Introduction to his 1907 book *How to Enjoy the Bible* wrote, "The root of all the evils which abound in the spiritual sphere at the present day lies in the fact that the Word and the words of God are not fed upon, digested, and assimilated, as they ought to be. If we ask the question, Why is this the case? The answer is, The Bible is not enjoyed **because the Bible is not understood.** The methods and rules by which alone such an understanding may be gained are not known or followed; hence the Bible is a neglected book." (Get a free copy of Bullinger's extensive book from markfoster.net/rn/how_to_enjoy_the_bible_bullinger.pdf.)

The story behind Jeremiah's enthusiastic statement (15:16) was the discovery during the reign of King Josiah of a scroll containing all or extracts from the first five books of the Old Testament (called the Pentateuch or Torah). The event is recorded in II Kings chapter 22. The temple was being repaired and the temple copy had been hidden when the building suffered damage by some marauding army perhaps some decades before.

Jeremiah said, *"Your words were found, and I ate them..."* The Bible often speaks of the believer being fed by the Word of God. For example, in Psalm 19:10 the words are said to be *"sweeter also than honey and drippings of the honeycomb."* Jesus quoted Deuteronomy 8:3: *"Man shall not live by bread alone, but by every word that comes from the mouth of God"* (Matthew 4:4; Luke 4:4). It was God's decision that He would use words to let humans know He exists and that He rewards those who diligently seek Him, as Hebrews 11:6 puts it. To eat the Word is to take it in and assimilate it. Unlike the unpleasant castor oil that my mother gave me every time I did not feel well, God's Word is food that produces joy and rejoicing, and therefore wise people devour it with great delight. *"When your words showed up, I ate them — swallowed them whole. What a feast!"* (MSG).

3
God's Thoughts and Our Thoughts

What is God's Word and why do we need to read it? Let's spend a few minutes answering those questions.

"For I know the thoughts that I have for you, says the Lord..." (Jeremiah 29:11). *"The Lord knows the thoughts of man..."* (Psalm 94:11). God has thoughts about you, but how do you know what He is thinking? We have thoughts, and God knows all of them! *"For as the heavens are higher than the earth, so are my ways higher than your ways and my thoughts than your thoughts"* (Isaiah 55:8).

Words are the clothes in which thoughts are dressed. You can only really know my thoughts if I put them into words. And you can only know God's thoughts if he puts them into words. That's why I prefer to use an "essentially literal" translation of God's Word, the Bible. A strictly literal translation would be very difficult to read because of the grammatical and word order differences between the languages. When Paul was brought before Gallio, the charge was dismissed because Gallio refused to judge on "a question of words and names" (Acts 18:15). But "words" are what the matter is all about.

Jesus declared, *"Man shall not live by bread alone,*

but by every word that comes from the mouth of God" (Matthew 4:4, Luke 4:4). And centuries before, the Psalmist recorded this immutable truth: *"The words of the Lord are pure words"* (Psalm 12:6). Timothy was exhorted to *"Hold fast the form of sound words"* (II Timothy 1:13). This form or pattern of sound words is essential to understanding divine truth.

It naturally follows that to have a pattern there must be underlying laws which give consistency and uniformity to a language. There are certain laws concerning biblical language that you should understand. **The first law** is the foundational law. *"All scripture is inspired by God"* (II Timothy 3:16). "Inspired by God" is the translation of one Greek word meaning "God-breathed." If we ignore this foundation even in a minute way, we fall prey to tradition rather than truth.

We must be totally convinced that God gave words to holy men of God, words they could understand and speak out or write down (II Peter 1:21, Galatians 1:11-12). God is the source of not only the Word of God but also the words used in the Word of God. A believer reading the sacred scriptures is either helped or hampered by his or her concept of them. If you or I consider Scripture as inspired, we become obligated to convey its thoughts with accuracy.

On the other hand, James Moffatt, author of the first popular paraphrase (1913), wrote: "Once the translator of the New Testament is freed from the influence of the theory of verbal inspiration,... difficulties cease to be so formidable." Thus if we are simply dealing with words written by fallible human writers, we are free to take many liberties to convey what we think they are trying to say. But what does the Word say: *"For no prophecy ever came*

14

by the will of a human, but holy men of God spoke being borne along by the Holy Spirit" (II Peter 1:21).

The second law of biblical language can be simply stated: No word is the exact equivalent of any other word. That is, the meaning or usage of one word is necessarily distinct from that of all other words. This is a remarkable though obvious law of language. God has no way to effectively communicate with us if he does not use words. And since He is the perfect, all-wise God, He uses words accurately and grammatically.

We may have opportunity to show in English some of the distinctions which the original language makes, and we must attempt to comprehend these distinctions. There are a multitude of tools to help us without having to learn biblical Hebrew or Greek.

The third law of biblical language takes us a step deeper into our quest for a "pattern of sound words": the meaning of a word is dependent on its usage. There are two stages in the meaning of a word. The root meaning which never varies, and the meaning derived from usage. For example, take the root verb "to act." A person who performs a deed is an "actor" or maybe an "activist." An act that was performed is a "fact." A building where people perform acts is called a "factory," and so forth.

The language you and I speak is a living language and the meanings derived from usage are changing all the time. The dictionaries we use are struggling to keep up-to-date. For example, the "by and by" (Luke 17:7) of the beloved 1611 KJV meant "immediately" when it was translated, not "sometime" as it means today.

The meaning of a biblical word will depend on how it is used in God's Word. "A text without a context is a pretext." Every context in which it occurs throws light upon its meaning. Thus the combined evidence of all its contexts fixes its meaning. We will then be able to see that special shading or coloring with which God clothed it. To adapt a well-known saying: the company a word keeps is an index of its character.

"How precious to me are your thoughts, O God! How vast is the sum of them! If I would count them, they are more than the sand" (Psalm 139:17-18a). Let's fall in love with the precious words that convey to us the thoughts of our loving Father God.

4

Man Shall Not Live by
Ice Cream Alone

The quote is based on the words Jesus found in both Matthew 4:4 and Luke 4:4, *"Man shall not live by bread alone, but by every word that comes from the mouth of God"* (ESV). And Jesus was quoting from the Old Testament book of Deuteronomy 8:3, so the truth has been applicable for millenniums! The Message Bible reads, *"It takes more than bread to stay alive. It takes a steady stream of words from God's mouth."*

I could paraphrase the text as "Man shall not live by Praise and Worship alone" if I wanted to emphasize the truth as applicable to today's expression of the church. In fact, you could replace any object and the truth that follows would still be valid.

It has been and always will be that without the Word of God taught faithfully and believed implicitly, humans have no foundation for victorious living in a hostile world. This is true from the Garden of Eden onwards. In the temptation of Eve, Satan said, *"Has God said?..."* He was questioning the integrity of God's Word and to this day people still question it or do not totally believe it.

Jesus taught his disciples that *"The words that I have spoken to you are spirit and life"* (John 6:63b). The rapid growth of the early church was because the apostles *"spoke the word of God with boldness"* (Acts 4:31); *"Now those who were scattered went about preaching the word"* (Acts 8:4). *"The next Sabbath almost the whole city gathered to hear the word of the Lord"* (Acts 12:24). There are only a few mentions of singing in Acts but many more accounts of God's Word being preached, believed, and acted upon.

This is why E.W. Kenyon wrote: "Here are some facts about the Word these men preached. It ruled their private lives. It was magnified. It increased; it grew, a living Power. It multiplied. Men were mastered by the Word. Men proclaimed the Word. Men gathered to hear the Word... The Word alone gave faith. The Word alone gave the New Birth. The Word alone gave healing. The Word alone bound the disciples together. That spoken Word that we see in the Book of Acts was the manna of God for the recreated human spirit. It still is" (from *Advanced Bible Studies*, Lesson 27).

Paul wrote to the Corinthians, *"I fed you with milk, not solid food, for you were not ready for it. And even now you are not yet ready"* (I Corinthians 3:2). The writer to the Hebrews penned, *"You have become dull of hearing. For though by this time you ought to be teachers, you need someone to teach you again the basic principles of the oracles of God [the ABCs]. You need milk, not solid food, for everyone who lives on milk is unskilled in the word of righteousness, since he is a child. But solid food is for the mature"* (Hebrews 5:11b-14a).

What do we see from all this? The Word was central in the early church. While the books of the New Testament had not started to be written until near the end of the Book of Acts, the disciples faithfully and boldly proclaimed what Jesus had taught, they majored on the resurrection of Jesus, and they ministered by the authority of his name. We now have the complete "New Testament" but the scriptures are no longer central to most churches or most believers.

To survive the coming storm, we will need to absolutely know that Christ is in us and we are in him. Start reinforcing these truths into your minds by reading, studying and understanding God's precious and powerful Word. *"By your words I can see where I'm going; they throw a beam of light on my dark path"* (Psalm 119:105 MSG).

5
There's More than One Way to Read the Bible

The previous chapters on enjoying the Bible can be summed up with these words: You will never "enjoy" the Bible if you read it as a discipline ("a verse a day keeps the devil away"); you will get excited when you simply read the words that are written because they taste good for your spirit. Remember Jeremiah, who wrote, *"Your words were found, and I ate them, and your words became to me a joy and the delight of my heart"* (Jeremiah 15:16)? Let's explore the ways in which you can read your Bible.

In the mid-1950s, before I went to Bible College, I purchased a 90-page paperback book titled *Enjoy Your Bible* by G.R. Harding-Wood of England. It cost me all of five shillings Australian (50 cents) and though it lost its front paper cover decades ago, I still refer to the book. It went through four editions (printings) in five years, so it was well received by those searching for help in enjoying their Bibles. In the second chapter the author makes four suggestions on turning your Bible reading from a duty to a joy. I am going to use his points as the framework for this discussion and add my own comments.

First, "How does a bride read a love letter? She read every word of it, that is, completely." *"God is love"* (I John 4:8) and *"God's love has been poured into our hearts"* (Romans 5:5), so the analogy is authentic. Yet "completely" is not how most people read their Bibles, our Father's love-letter to us.

I've made the point for many years that we should remember that each book of the Bible was written to be read from start to finish. It was not written with the concept of taking a sentence out of the middle and one near the end. When Paul wrote his letters to the young churches, I can see a gathering of believers sitting there listening carefully to every word, even though *"there are some things in them that are hard to understand"* (II Peter 3:16).

Often when I went overseas on my own to teach, my wife Vivien would sneak a letter into my suitcase, to remind me of our love for each other. I still have some of those letters. Every word in them was important to me. I'd read them several times and smile. I would also receive a mailed letter from her at my second or third speaking appointment, also written before I left home.

So the point is, your love for the Author of the Bible determines your attitude towards the words you are reading. How important are they to you? We are to live by *"every word that comes from the mouth of God"* (Matthew 4:4, Luke 4:4); Jesus was quoting Deuteronomy 8:3). We will discover later that it is the little one-syllable words we all know that are the most important.

Second, "How does a traveller consult a road map? The answer is constantly." We are pilgrims, travellers on a journey to a place prepared for us on the right hand of the Father. We have a passport that gains us entry into heaven. We sing, "This world is not my home, I'm just a passing through..." In past days we would have a map that would tell us everything we wanted to know (except how to fold it up again!). If we weren't sure which road to take while travelling, we would get the map out and check it before proceeding. Now new cars have a GPS unit that talks to us constantly about where to go next, unless you have wisely found out how to mute it.

I encourage you to go straight to the source, the Bible, constantly. Check up on what people tell you. Be like the Bereans who heard Paul and *"they received the word with all eagerness, examining the Scriptures daily to see if these things were so"* (Acts 17:11). Even watching Christian TV, when a speaker comes out with a debatable statement, Vivien and I say, "Book, chapter, and verse, please!" So "read the Bible completely; consult it constantly."

Third, "How does a scholar study a lesson book? The answer is carefully." *"Do your best to present yourself to God as one approved, a worker who has no need to be ashamed, rightly handling the word of truth"* (II Timothy 2:15). The word translated "study" in the KJV and "do your best" in the ESV, is "to be earnest" or "to be diligent," and that takes some effort.

For example, Paul was careful to point out that a particular word was singular and not plural in Galatians 3:16, *"Now the promises were made to Abraham and to his offspring. It does not say, 'And to offsprings,' referring to many, but referring to one, 'And to your offspring,' who is Christ."*

In the first chapter of this book, "The Lord is My Shepherd," I demonstrated how carefully noting the personal pronouns "he" and "me" puts the emphasis on the relationship between God and me and clarifies how it works out in everyday life.

Fourth, **"How does a good soldier obey Army orders? The answer is conscientiously."** Of course, we're talking about God's orders to us here, not denominational directions or the pastor's insistence. The distinction is not always clear. The psalmist wrote, "*Your commandment makes me wiser than my enemies, for it is ever with me.* [99]*I have more understanding than all my teachers, for your testimonies are my meditation*" (Psalm 119:98-99). The whole of Psalm 119 is about God's Word. Jesus revealed that "*the Father who sent me has himself given me a commandment—what to say and what to speak.*" On the night before he died, he told his disciples, "*I do as the Father has commanded me*" (John 14:31b).

Let's give the final word to G.R. Harding-Wood: "Practise, then,

Reading the Bible completely like a love-letter,
Consulting it constantly like a road-map,
Studying it carefully like a lesson book, and
Obeying it conscientiously like Army orders."

23

6
Don't Lose What
God Reveals to You

As you are reading your Bible at home you might see something about the words that strike you as interesting, or you are listening to a teaching and as you follow it in your Bible something catches your attention. This is the Spirit of God pointing to something He wants you to understand. *"No one comprehends the thoughts of God except the Spirit of God. [12]Now we have received not the spirit of the world, but the Spirit who is from God, that we might understand the things freely given us by God"* (I Corinthians 2:11b-12).

Now be honest, will you remember what it was that caught your attention a day later? Will you remember where in the Word it was? D.L. Moody, the "Billy Graham" of the late 1800s, wrote in his book *Golden Counsels* (1899), "Unless you have an uncommon memory, you cannot retain the good things you hear. If you trust to your ear alone, they will escape you in a day or two; but, if you mark your Bible, and enlist the aid of your eye, you will never lose them."

So let's talk about Bible marking, a common practice in Moody's day but rarely mentioned now. Today in many churches the scripture texts are placed on a screen, enhancing the "spectator" attitude to the service and giving the impression that you don't need a Bible; "come just as you are!" But as a young Christian, I saw many fellow believers write in their Bibles. In 2004 I was privileged to inspect the KJV Bible used by Bible teacher E.W. Kenyon, and it was well marked. Moody wisely wrote, "Do not buy a Bible that you are unwilling to mark and use."

My own KJV Bible that I've used for over 50 years is marked, particularly in books like Ephesians where the pages are grubby and ready to fall out. I notice that I used fine ballpoint pens (not gel ink), red, green, and blue in color, to contrast with the black type, and also some pencil marks, a soft 2B. A large-print Bible, say 9.1/4" x 6", is best because you can write words between the lines. I have a new identical Bible sitting on my shelf with real leather binding, but I can't face the task of transferring all my notes! As Charles Spurgeon said, "A Bible that's falling apart usually belongs to someone who isn't!" You can also buy wide-margin Bibles, also known as journaling Bibles.

I mentioned before that a "literal" translation is best for study, such as the ESV, NKJV, NASB or KJV, while a paraphrase or mixture of both has value for illustrative purposes. I'm not a "King James Only" teacher, but the KJV has the most reference works published in any version.

It's time for some examples. I'm concentrating on the words in the Word, not on topics. There are many suggested systems that assign a color to a topic. The problem is your Bible will start to look like a rainbow and it is difficult to remember which topic goes with a specific color. I suggest that you change your reading style for a while from reading by topics to reading the books of the Bible as they were written, chapter by chapter.

Suppose you decide to read through Ephesians in the KJV, and you begin with chapter one verse one. You notice the two "in" prepositions and question this. The saints are both *"in Ephesus"* and *"in Christ Jesus;"* in two positions or locations at the one time (see page 168, *Completely Satisfied in Christ* by Peter Wade). You could perhaps underline the two "in's" or circle them. Of course, some people have digital versions and you'll have to work out for yourself how to mark the text, perhaps highlighting or underlining. So, that's an example of a repetition of words in the same verse.

Later you read verses 18-19 of chapter 1, *"Having the eyes of your hearts enlightened, that you may know..."* (ESV). There are two "what" words in the rest of the verse and another one in verse 19. Each usage signifies the start of an indirect question, so you could place the numbers 1, 2, and 3 in front of each "what" respectively. You can know in reality these three great truths. In fact, your heart (the seat of your personal life in your brain) has been enlightened so you can know these things. That's an example of a list, but it is not clearly seen in the way the type is set in your Bible until you mark it.

There's another list in Ephesians chapter 2, verses 5 and 6. "Dead," "made alive," "raised," and "seated."

Another technique is called a "railway connection" (or "tram lines" in the UK and Australia), a thin line underlining one statement and then connected to the start of the underline of a second statement. In KJV Ephesians chapter 2, verse 2, *"in time past;"* verse 3, *"in times past;"* verse 11, *"in time past;"* and then verse 13, *"But now..."* Or you could circle the phrase and join the two usages.

You can read Moody's full article online at www.peterwade.com/article/other/bible-marking-moody.

7
Is Every Promise in the Book Mine?

In our quest to enjoy the Bible, I have quoted the saying, "The Bible is not enjoyed because it is not understood" (E.W. Bullinger). And to understand the Bible we'll need to jettison some false concepts that have come to us through lyrics of choruses and song, as well as those from false teachings, and even from the way the English Bible is laid out.

In the second church we pastored in Western Australia, the start of the Sunday evening service was usually comprised of singing choruses from the yellow *Elim Choruses* words-only edition. One I remember was No. 636: "Every promise in the Book is mine, Every chapter, every verse, every line, All the blessings of His love divine, Every promise in the Book is mine." And in our ignorance we'd sing it with vigor.

Just because you sing or hear a song doesn't make it truth for you! Take this promise: *"Every place that the sole of your foot will tread upon I have given to you"* (Joshua 1:3). Look out Warren Buffett and Bill Gates! I'm passing your net worth at rocket speed! Just because someone prayed *"Search me, O God"* in Psalm 139:23 doesn't mean we now have to sing the prayer "Search me, O God, and know my heart today." God already knows you heart! *"You, Lord, who know the hearts of all*" (Acts 1:24). The chorus above cannot be true because God made many promises to individuals and nations in the Old Testament that were specific to them and not to you and me.

To understand the Bible, we should first consider what it is. We see it as one book because that is how our English translation is bound. In reality it is a collection of 66 books, 39 in the Old Testament and 27 in the New Testament. It was penned by around 33 writers over a period of about 1,500 years. It is conveniently divided into two parts: the "Old Covenant," later known as the "Old Testament," which was primarily written in Hebrew, and the "New Testament," primarily written in Greek.

Between the two testaments was a period when no books were penned, probably around 350 years or so. For our convenience, there is a title page placed between the two testaments yet totally without divine inspiration, and it is the most confusing page of the whole Bible! It reads: "The New Testament of our Lord and Savior Jesus Christ."

"For where a will is involved, the death of the one who made it must be established. For a will takes effect only at death, since it is not in force as long as the one who made it is alive" (Hebrews 9:16-17). Yes, it will be shock to many to discover that the New Testament, Will, or Covenant (all the same Greek word) does not start at Matthew 1:1. It can only start at the death of Jesus!

"First, the New Testament doesn't actually begin in Matthew 1. In fact, it doesn't begin at any page in the Bible. It begins at the point in history when Jesus' blood was shed. No blood was shed in the first chapter of Matthew, and no sacrificial death was carried out in the manger. It was not our Savior's birth that changed everything. It was his death that inspired the apostles to declare the message of 'out with the old, and in with the new'" (Andrew Farley, *The Naked Gospel*, 2008, page 80).

He goes on to observe, "When we attempt to mix Old with New, we end up with a contradictory covenant of our own invention. This is where I lived for years. Since there were a few elements of the New in my imaginary covenant, it didn't kill me right away. Instead, it afforded me a slower death. I had adopted a belief system that was essentially a balance of Old and New. I neither suffered under the stringency of the entire law nor enjoyed the bliss of unconditional favor."

So the Past must not be read into the Present, the Present is not to be read into the Past, and the Future is not to be read into the Present, as E.W. Bullinger details in 60+ pages of his book "How to Enjoy the Bible." I have often stated that my ministry is for "generic New Testament Christians." "Generic" means not specific or having no brand name, and "New Testament" because in reality those are the only kind of Christians who exist!

"The New is in the Old concealed; the Old is in the New revealed" (one of the few quotes from St. Augustine that I agree with!). So there is value in the Old, but we're living in the New in Acts 29 territory (since the church age didn't end with Acts 28:31, the last narrative section of the New Testament).

Even in the ministry of Jesus there are contradictory statements that are only understood by noting when they were spoken. In Luke 9:3 when sending out the twelve disciples to minister, *"And he said to them, Take nothing for your journey, no staff, nor bag, nor bread, nor money; and do not have two tunics."* Yet just before Jesus died he said to them, *"'When I sent you out with no moneybag or knapsack or sandals, did you lack anything?' They said, 'Nothing.' *[36]*He said to them, 'But now let the one who has a moneybag take it, and likewise a knapsack. And let the one who has no sword sell his cloak and buy one'"* (Luke 22:35b-36). Notice the "But now..." So the new command cancels the old. And many Old Testament promises and commands are replaced by New Testament commands and promises.

Is there an answer to this situation that you can understand? Yes, there is! It is to take notice of the address on the envelope.

8
The Address on the Envelope

When I started work I was an "office boy," now known as a P.A., personal assistant, I picked up the mail at the central post office in the morning. In those days most of the letters were addressed to "The Manager." In the vast majority of cases those letters addressed to the manager were of great interest to others. Yet many managers got quite upset if someone else read the letters before they did. Nowadays, even though my wife Vivien and I have joint accounts, privacy laws insist we each have to receive a statement in a separate envelope, one addressed to me and one to Vivien.

It is now, in fact, against the law to open another person's mail. So look at **the address on the envelope**. Does it have your name on the outside? If it does, then what it says is specifically for you. If your name is not on the envelope, it is not specifically for you but you may learn some things from its contents if it is shown to you. Often the only way you can resolve an apparent contradiction in the Bible is to apply this filter.

Not all of the 66 books of the Bible have your name on them, but you can learn something from all of them. Miles Cloverdale, in his 1535 English translation of the New

Testament, wrote about studying the Bible: "It shall greatly help ye to understand Scripture, if thou mark not only what is spoken or written, but of whom, and to whom..." and seven other rules. These wise words have helped Christians for nearly 500 years. The "to whom" is of interest to us at this point.

Romans 15:4 will help you to understand this concept. (The statement follows a quotation in verse 3 from Psalm 69:9.) *"For whatever things were written before were written for our learning, so that we through endurance and comfort of the Scriptures might have expectation."* Romans is a book in the church period, and so what was written before that time is "for our learning." It will not be addressed to us but it was written to teach us.

The same concept is stated in I Corinthians 10:11: *"Now these things happened to them as examples, and they were written down for our instruction, on whom the end of the ages has come."* The previous ten verses quote examples from the history of the nation of Israel. What happened to Moses and to the nation have been written down so that we can be instructed by their example.

In I Corinthians 10:32 we have God's three-fold classification of all people: *"Give no offense to Jews or to Greeks or to the church of God."* The church of God is not made up of Jews or Greeks (non-Jews), but it is made up of Christians: *"There is neither Jew nor Greek... for you are all one in Christ Jesus"* (Galatians 3:28). For each of these three groups of people God has a plan, God has promises to fulfill for them. God addresses Himself to them in the various books of the Bible and occasionally in a specific portion of a book. What He says to Jewish people may or may not be of interest to the church. God said some very strong words to nations other than Israel, and we would hope those words were not meant for us! To be sure if it is meant for you, read the address on the envelope.

To whom is it written? Let me give some examples. The first words of the book of Isaiah are these: *"The vision of Isaiah the son of Amoz, which he saw concerning Judah and Jerusalem..."* (Isaiah 1:1). That is the "address" or title on the envelope. Isaiah contains "the vision... concerning Judah and Jerusalem." So there is no doubt about the "to whom," but we can learn many things from Isaiah that do concern us as Christians, like the coming Messiah of Isaiah 53.

In the New Testament, the book of James is addressed... *"To the twelve tribes in the dispersion"* (1:1). The twelve tribes are the Jews, and God had some special things to say to them at that time in their history. There are things I can learn from the book of James but it is not written to the church. Many of the books of the Bible are written for someone else but are also helpful for our learning.

Other books are written to us, to the church. Let's check a few of these. I Corinthians is addressed... *"To the church of God that is in Corinth, to those sanctified in Christ Jesus, called saints with all those who in every place call upon the name of our Lord, Jesus Christ, both theirs and ours"* (1:2). We are included in the address on the envelope! It is written to the church.

Ephesians is addressed... *"To the saints in Ephesus, the faithful in Christ Jesus"* (1:1). I praise God that I am one of the "faithful in Christ Jesus"; my name is on the envelope. Romans through II Thessalonians are the letters addressed to the seven churches, and all have our name on the envelope. Then follow some "pastoral epistles" written to individuals in the same church period, and they too contain truth that applies to us, right up to Philemon.

Now which books do you think we ought to read first? Which books should we "correctly cut," "rightly divide" (II Timothy 2:15) in order to be approved to God? Yes, the ones that are addressed to us. Those books are "a curriculum which contains everything necessary for the Christian's standing and his walk," as E.W. Bullinger so accurately states in his book *The Church Epistles*.

This is why I have taught the book of Revelation only twice in sixty years of ministry. It is not important to know the meaning of the hair on the end of the horn of the seven-horned beast that rises out of the sea, as recorded in the book of Revelation. It is really important to know what it means to be "in Christ" and "as Christ" in this world, and know "Christ in you."

How God works now may be different from how He worked for Israel in Old Testament times, and in some ways it may be the same. I will only know if an Old Testament verse has meaning for me when I compare it to what God says on the same subject in those books addressed to me. The same is true of what is written in the Gospels. When someone asks me what a Bible verse means, the first thing I do is to check the address on the envelope, and in many cases that solves the apparent difficulty.

This principle demands that I be diligent by correctly cutting, rightly dividing the word of truth. To do this I must apply the concept that the Bible interprets itself, often right where it is written. In addition, I must check the address on the envelope and ensure that it was written specifically to me. Since I want to enjoy positive living, I need the sure foundation of God's positive Word and apply its truth to my life.

[The title of this chapter comes from a booklet by A.E. Knoch, the compiler of the Concordant Literal Version (NT).

9
A Steady Stream of Words

In my last chapter I made the point that some scripture is written directly to the church age in which we live, as shown by "the address on the envelope," but we can learn from the parts addressed to other groups. Before we go deeper into the books addressed to us, let's look at the rest of the Bible.

In a quirk of verse numbering by Robert Estienne in 1555, both Matthew 4:4 and Luke 4:4 contain essentially the same words of Jesus. *"It is written, 'Man shall not live by bread alone, but by every word that comes from the mouth of God."* The Message paraphrase reads, *"It takes more than bread to stay alive. It takes a steady stream of words from God's mouth."*

Jesus was being tempted by Satan and in reply is quoting directly from Deuteronomy 8:3: *"And he [God] humbled you and let you hunger and fed you with manna, which you did not know, nor did your fathers know, that he might make you know that man does not live by bread alone, but man lives by every word that comes from the mouth of the Lord."*

One commentary says, "Now, if Israel spent, not forty days, but forty years in a waste, howling wilderness, where there were no means of human subsistence, not starving, but divinely provided for, on purpose to prove to every age that human support depends not upon bread, but upon God's unfailing word of promise and pledge of all needful providential care, am I, distrusting this word of God, and despairing of relief, to take the law into My own hand?" (Jamieson, Fausset and Brown).

So let's get the impact of "*every word.*" Our personal faith is encouraged and strengthened by "every word" in the scriptures, "a steady stream of words," so long as we partake of them. Jeremiah discovered a missing parchment and he wrote, "*Your words were found, and I ate them, and your words became to me a joy and the delight of my heart*" (Jeremiah 15:16). One preacher put it something like this, "You can't live on just one cold meal on Sunday morning and nothing the rest of the week, and expect your faith to work." You need a "steady stream" of "every word."

This is why there are so many daily devotional books on the market. People like to read just one verse and then someone's comment on it. That's a good place to start, but I'd rather encourage you to get a daily reading chart, like one that has you reading the whole New Testament in one year. Here's one that is free which you can download and print out: www.peterwade.com/wp-content/uploads/newtestament _yearly.pdf.

Many of us were blessed to be brought up in a home where the Bible was believed, like Timothy in the New Testament. "*I am reminded of your sincere faith, a faith that dwelt first in your grandmother Lois and your mother Eunice and now, I am sure, dwells in you as well*" (II Timothy 1:5). "*And that from a child thou hast known the holy scriptures, which are able to make thee wise unto salvation through faith which is in Christ Jesus. *[16]*All **scripture** is inspired by God, and* *is profitable for teaching, for reproof, for correction, and for training in righteousness, ¹⁷that the man of God may be equipped, fitted out for every good act"* (II Timothy 3:15-17).

In verse 16 we have the phrase *"All scripture is inspired by God"* ["God-breathed"]. This is the same truth as in Matthew 4:4, *"... every word that proceeds out of the mouth of God."* Then in II Timothy we are told this scripture is "profitable..." for four purposes which enable us to be equipped for every thing that we will ever run across. These purposes are teaching, reproof, correction, and training in righteousness, and we need all of them!

So enjoy your Bible, every word of it, not just on Sundays but 24/7, as modern street language terms it.

10
The Training of the Twelve

Let's look at the four Gospels: Matthew, Mark, Luke, and John. Since no gospel has our "address on the envelope," what value do they have for the church today? They are of great value, is the simple answer.

The four gospels are part of the transition from the Jewish history and relationship with God to the new Christian age and a new relationship to God. Much of the gospels are teaching and demonstrating the coming church age, the age of the Holy Spirit. My title for this chapter is the title of the 1871 classic book by Alexander Bruce which is still in print, and emphasises "how Jesus the Master Trainer prepared his tiny band of followers to win the world with faith and love." (Available in paperback at Amazon.com.

The internal evidence in the gospels is strong for this viewpoint. Let's notice first the integrity and veracity of the words of Jesus. "*Whoever does not love me does not keep my words. And the word that you hear is not mine but the Father's who sent me*" (John 14:10b also verse 24). These verses teach us that the Father God was always feeding Jesus the words He wanted him to say. That statement alone shows how much notice we should take of them.

Yet it goes beyond just words, as we see in John 5:19b, *"The Son can do nothing of his own accord, but only what he sees the Father doing. For whatever the Father does, that the Son does likewise."* And also verse 36: *"For the works that the Father has given me to accomplish, the very works that I am doing, bear witness about me that the Father has sent me."* Not only words, but works also. So everything Jesus said and did came direct from the Father. God was "training the twelve" through the ministry of Jesus. To my mind, that has to be the best training a minister of the gospel could ever receive.

While Jesus was a great orator who could hold a crowd in his hand (*"And the great throng heard him gladly"* Mark 12:37b), he used many methods to train his disciples. Take, for example, the record of feeding the 5,000, the only miracle reported in all four gospels apart from the resurrection. When Jesus saw the great crowd following him, *"Jesus said to Philip, 'Where are we to buy bread, so that these people may eat?' ⁶He said this to test him, for he himself knew what he would do"* (John 6:5b-6).

So this was "work experience" for the disciples on a grand scale. Jesus wanted to demonstrate that they needed to trust him to supply all their need at all times. Whether it was just his own small evangelistic team, who were well take care of — *"... And the twelve were with him, ²and also some women who had been healed... ³and many others, who provided for them out of their means"* (see Luke 8:1-3) — or 5,000 men plus women and children, the disciples had to learn the life of faith, not fund-raising. Today the church has reversed this, to its harm.

Jesus used a similar method when he sent out the twelve and then the seventy to preach and heal the sick. *"Acquire no gold nor silver nor copper for your belts, [10]no bag for your journey, nor two tunics nor sandals nor a staff, for the laborer deserves his food"* (Matthew 10:9-10 ESV). Today we would say he threw them in at the deep end! Yet they found that faith in his words worked! *"And he said to them, 'When I sent you out with no moneybag or knapsack or sandals, did you lack anything?' They said, 'Nothing.'"* (Luke 22:35).

At other times, Jesus would take his disciples aside after preaching to the masses, and explain the stories he had used and their application to the disciples. Two examples among many: *"And when he had entered the house and left the people, his disciples asked him about the parable"* (Mark 7:17), and he told them. Also Matthew 20:17, while walking along the road to Jerusalem, *"And as Jesus was going up to Jerusalem, he took the twelve disciples aside, and on the way he said to them..."*

Fifteen times in the Gospels Jesus said, *"But I say unto you"* (KJV). In the Sermon on the Mount in Matthew chapter 5, Jesus uses those words six times, on each occasion first quoting an Old Testament truth or a tradition added to the written law by the legalistic Jews, and then he would say *"but I say unto you,"* and refocused their thinking on the God of love and mercy Who revealed Himself in the Old Testament. The structure of these fifteen occasions is that you were taught something by man but God has already taught you the opposite. Tradition versus truth, and truth wins every time!

Jesus also said *"Do not think that I have come to abolish the Law or the Prophets; I have not come to abolish them but to fulfill them"* (Matthew 5:17). And he did fulfill all the requirements of the Mosiac Law on the cross of Calvary, and the veil of the temple was split in two, demonstrating the old Mosiac law was no longer needed to have a close relationship with God. Jesus also said, *"I am come that they might have life, and that they might have it more abundantly"* (John 10:10b KJV). *"I came so they can have real and eternal life, more and better life than they ever dreamed of"* (MSG).

However, not everything that Jesus said can be taken over into the church age. He spoke some pretty harsh words to the religionists of his day. He called them vipers, serpents (Matthew 12:34) and said they were of their father the devil (John 8:44), so it is wise to take notice of the context and to whom he was speaking. On his last night before he was crucified, John chapters 14 to 17 contain many wonderful truths that were not applicable right then but are now since the Holy Spirit was given to believers on the Day of Pentecost.

"And I will ask the Father, and he will give you another Helper, to be with you forever, [17]even the Spirit of truth, whom the world cannot receive, because it neither sees him nor knows him. You know him, for he dwells with you and will be in you" (John 14:16-17). And the "Comforter (Counselor, Helper, Intercessor, Advocate, Strengthener, and Standby)" (AMP) is in you and will abide forever.

Perhaps you're starting to see why we should not only enjoy the books of the Bible that are addressed to us (the letters to the seven churches in particular) but also the five narrative books that came before them in the New Testament, since while they are transitional in closing out the Old Covenant they give insight into how the Father sees the life of the believers after the Day of Pentecost.

11
The Young Church in Action

I now move on to **The Acts of the Apostles,** as it is titled in
our English Bibles. Actually it is mostly about two apostles:
Peter and Paul. Our lecturer during ministerial training told
us the title should be "The Acts of the Holy Spirit," but maybe
that was a touch of Pentecostal enthusiasm, yet I have since
found out it is the title of a book by A.T. Pierson. Actually a
number of manuscripts just title it as "Acts."

"Now many signs and wonders were regularly done
among the people by the hands of the apostles" (Acts 5:12),
so it would be better to say that it was a "divine-human
reciprocity" (Oral Roberts). Others say it this way: "Without
you, God will not, and without Him, you cannot." So let's
look at the fifth narrative book of the New Testament.

We have seen that some books have our "address on the
envelope," such as Paul's writings, and these should
predominantly be our source of faith and practice. Other
books are written for our learning, and in our last chapter we
looked at the four Gospels. Jesus instructed his disciples on
many things, but not about everything that was about to
happen. This was intentional, as they had to rely upon the
power of the Holy Spirit and the Christ within for their

guidance in the situations they ran across, in other words, they had to live by faith. Sometimes they used their sanctified imagination until they really learned the lesson to only do what they were guided to do, just as Jesus only did and said what the Father told him.

In the circles in which I first ministered, everyone wanted to get back to the "early church," by which they meant Acts chapters 2-4. However, if you want the early church, you have to take Acts chapter 5 also, the account of Ananias trying to mislead God in financial matters and coming off second best, dying when confronted with the truth. Few of my fellow worshippers were in favor of going that literal!

The apostles at first attempted to overlay the new spirit-filled Christian teaching on the foundation of the Jewish faith, as seen in the early chapters of Acts up until about chapter 10 and the conversion of Cornelius, but against great opposition from the religionists. One author I just read in *Ministry Today* wrote: "The New Testament and Old Testament are organically connected together with the New building upon the Old, not eradicating it altogether!"

However, Jesus said you cannot put new wine into old bottles, and we've already discussed that the New Testament started when the testator died, which meant the old order was finished. Yes, there is much of the Old Testament in the new, but there is much more that is now irrelevant. By Acts 13:46 the apostles ceased trying to convert those of the Jewish faith and mostly ministered to other nations—*"we turn to the Gentiles."* They themselves, however, still wanted to participate in Jewish worship, as seen with Paul hurrying to Jerusalem to celebrate the Feast of Pentecost (Acts 20:16).

The book of Acts is a **transistional** book — that's the important lesson. The Mosiac Law was gradually replaced by the grace of God, the outward rituals replaced by faith in Christ. Peter and John still went up to the temple every day to pray (Acts 3:1), and even as late as Acts 16:3, *"Paul wanted Timothy to accompany him, and he took him and circumcised him because of the Jews who were in those places, for they all knew that his father was a Greek."* This was like a Baptist learning when to kneel and when to do the sign of the cross so they wouldn't look out of place at a Roman Catholic Mass!

Division between Christians and the Jewish faith started to show long before Paul's second missionary journey, for Acts 6:7 tells us that *"a great company of the priests were obedient to the faith,"* and later at Antioch after a stirring sermon by Paul in the synagogue, *"Now when the congregation was broken up, many of the Jews and religious proselytes followed Paul and Barnabas: who, speaking to them, persuaded them to continue in the grace of God"* (Acts 13:43).

There is just so much that we can learn from the early church in the first 33 years as given in Acts, and learning brings with it enjoyment and a responsibility to follow the examples set before us.

The record of the early church in the book of Acts sets a great example before us. Here are just a few verses that tend to stand out for me. Acts 2:42 says about the 3,000 saved on the Day of Pentecost, *"And they devoted themselves to the apostles' teaching and the fellowship, to the breaking of bread and the prayers."* This is what believers should still be doing. Acts 3:6 records Peter saying to the lame man at the temple gate, *"Such as I have give I thee"* (KJV). What did Peter have? It met the lame man's need and through it the needs of many. You'd better find out what Peter had because you have it too!

When Peter and John were arrested and questioned about the healing, the record observes, *"Now when they [the priests] saw the boldness of Peter and John, and perceived that they were uneducated, common men, they were astonished. And they recognized that they had been with Jesus"* (Acts 4:13). It is better to have been with Jesus and stay unlearned and ignorant (KJV) than have a parchment on the wall saying you have been ordained! As two young people with the call of God on us to go into ministry, we heard a wise Bible College president say, "It's better to go to Calvary and miss college, than go to college and miss Calvary."

Acts 4:33 reports, *"And with great power the apostles were giving their testimony to the resurrection of the Lord Jesus, and great grace was upon them all."* The message of the early church was about the resurrection of Jesus, and because He lives, you too can live!

Read the Acts of the Apostles from start to finish, and rejoice that this is the church universal of which you are a part.

12
Paul, the Letter Writer

Paul wrote 14 books of the New Testament (about half), although one book does not bear his name but many scholars consider it was written by him (Hebrews). Most are letters he wrote to various churches and individuals. Some are more like textbooks, like Romans and Hebrews.

Romans to Second Thessalonians are called the "letters to the seven churches," and these are followed by four letters to people, collectively known as the "pastoral epistles," followed by the book of Hebrews, written predominantly to the Jewish people but with some areas especially for the gentiles or non-Jewish people.

Both E.W. Bullinger and E.W. Kenyon are correct in asserting that the Pauline revelation found in his writings are specifically for the church age, and are addressed to us as "the faithful in Christ Jesus" (Ephesians 1:1). These contain the final gospel for our time, and take precedence over other parts of the Bible. We may also include the pastoral letters from I Timothy to Philemon, since they come from the same time-frame. See the article "The Four Gospels in Contrast with the Pauline Epistles" by E.W. Kenyon on our website.

The order in which Paul's writings appear in our English

Bibles and most extant Greek manuscripts is called the canonical order, and for a long period I believed the theory that it was the divine order and had meaning. I have written about my change of belief in my article "The Church Epistles and E.W. Bullinger" on our website. The theory *may* have come from a fellow Anglican minister, Thomas Bernard, who in 1864 delivered a series of lecture called "the Bampton lectures" and later released them in a book in 1872 titled *The Progress of Doctrine in the New Testament*.

However, the method used to order Paul's letters is actually the same as used in the Old Testament for the Major Prophets and the Minor Prophets. It is based on the number of lines (*stichos*, Greek) in the manuscripts, from the longest book down to the shortest. A good explanation is given on Wikipedia under the title Stichometry. A fuller treatment can be found in the 1995 book *Paul the Letter-Writer* by Jerome Murphy-O'Connor, from which the title of this chapter has come. I will leave you to check out the above material if you are interested.

One final comment is necessary on the position of Hebrews as the last document in Paul's writing, and the explanation is simple. As the only document not bearing Paul's name within it, the group of scholars confirming its place in the collection decided to place it after Paul's named letters.

I have published books on Ephesians and Colossians, and constantly encourage believers to read and believe what all the letters to the seven churches teach. As Bullinger wrote: "The Church Epistles are the complete course which shall begin and finish the education of the Christian."

13
Big Words and Little Words

Now that we have completed our birds-eye view of the Bible, it is time to get to the actual text. In the first two chapters I counselled you to **just read what is written**, like you would any other book.

Here is a statement from a church website that is well worth quoting: "From our belief in an intelligent, loving Creator, we should expect God to reveal His message in writing, the historic medium best suited for precision, preservation, and propagation" (author unknown). God gave us in the Bible an absolute and specific record of His will for the human race, which we call "our sole guide for faith and practice."

In Australia, for example, the Aboriginal people have an oral and pictorial record of their history in this land, but not a written history until European settlement in the late 1700s. Therefore they rely on their elders to interpret the oral and pictorial accounts to each new generation. Given that English is a living language, we have a constant stream of new translations and paraphrases to help each new generation understand the word and will of God.

So with the background I have laid out for you, I will start sharing some of the "methods and rules" that scholars have suggested over the centuries.

Many people imagine that preachers go to a seminary or Bible College to understand the big words of our faith and learn how to teach them to the people. Yes there are big, multi-syllable words in the Bible that translators have used to embody aspects of our faith, like righteousness and sanctification and so forth. The longest word in the KJV is actually the name of Isaiah's son, Maher-shalal-hash-baz (Isaiah 8:3). Theologians also seem to love big words to describe teachings, for example, antinomianism, trinitarian, supersessionism and plenty of others.

Big words do have their place but it is the little words that are the driving force of our language and give the accuracy English needs. *"For God so loved the world, that He gave his only son, that whoever believes in him should not perish but have eternal life"* (John 3:16). There are mainly small words in that verse, but it is a big truth!

I first understood the importance of little words from a Christian magazine article in the early 1960s titled "Little Words of Great Meaning" by Henry Jacobsen, with examples from the Bible, and the article filled in a gap in my broken education. To take little words to the extreme, I have a magazine article in my library solely on the use of the article "a" and "the" in the Greek text!

In his book *A Man in Christ* (1935), James Stewart writes, "It was a dictum of Luther's that all religion lies in the pronouns... But Deissmann, going a step further than Luther, has virtually declared that religion resides in the prepositions, and in one of them in particular" (pp. 154-155). The particular one is "in," as used in the phrase *"in Christ Jesus."* E. Stanley Jones wrote, "Obviously this 'in' brings us nearer than 'near Christ,' 'following Christ,' 'believing in Christ,' or even 'committed to Christ.' You cannot go further or deeper than 'in.'" Can you see the power of one little word?

My favorite example of pronouns comes from Ephesians 1:4, *"Even as he [God] chose us [the saints, the faithful] in him [in Christ Jesus]..."* Who said Bible study is always difficult and dull? "He, us, and him" sums up the whole scope of theology. The relationships make a winning combination! Jesus taught, *"I in them and you in me, that they may become perfectly one"* (John 17:23). We read how wealthy we are in Christ Jesus from Ephesians 1:4-14, said to be the longest sentence in the New Testament, yet we can understand it from the little words.

For an example of prepositions, we need to look no further than Ephesians 1:1, *"To the saints who are in Ephesus, and faithful in Christ Jesus."* This is the address on the envelope and the preposition "in" appears twice, for we are indeed in two places at the one time! "Coming to grips with the paradox of being in two locations is perhaps the most important thing we can do as Christian believers. You probably have no doubt where you are right now as you read this, as far as physical location is concerned, but are you convinced that you are 'in Christ Jesus' at this very moment too?" (from chapter 68, *Completely Satisfied in Christ* by Peter Wade).

For those who fell asleep in English grammar classes, pronouns are words that substitute for a noun or noun phrase, like "me," "who," "you," "it," and so forth. Prepositions ("to put before") are words that express space or time relationships with the word that follows, like "in," "under," "towards," "before." And that's as deep as we need to get into grammar. For a full description of prepositions in the New

Testament, read this extract from the Companion Bible at www.levendwater.org/companion/append104.html .

Even simple words of connection like "and" (known as conjunctions: "and," "but," "yet," "when") have great importance. We often forget that the Bible was originally handwritten on scrolls, and the Greek was in all capital letters with no spaces between words and no punctuation! And there were no italics or bold faces to use either, so any emphasis had to be supplied by the words used. I'll conclude this short summary with the use and non-use of the word "and."

When no "ands" are used in a list, we are not to stop and consider the particulars but to hasten on to the grand climax. When many "ands" are used there is no climax and we should read slowly, weighing each item that is presented and consider each particular that is emphasized by the "and." To see this in an English translation you will need an essentially literal version like KJV, NKJV, NASB, ESV, etc.

Take Luke chapter 14 where both types of lists appear. In verses 13-14a we have no "ands": *"But when you give a feast, invite the poor, the crippled, the lame, the blind, ¹⁴and you will be blessed..."* We should not stop to consider the plight of those listed but to hurry on to the conclusion, *"and you will be blessed."*

In verse 21 regarding another great banquet when no invitees came, the angry master commands his servant, *"Go out quickly to the streets and lanes of the city, and bring in the poor and crippled and blind and lame..."* Here we need to stop and think about each of the people mentioned and how we can minister to them. Some translations even add commas to further slow down our reading.

So the lesson here is to **take notice of the little words** and the impact they have on the subject matter. In doing so you will find that the big words become easier to understand. Actually the big words are usually compound words anyway—combinations of little words! When you see a little word that opens up some truth to you, **mark** your Bible! Underline it, circle it, highlight it. Little words do have great jobs to do in God's Word.

14
You and the Box

I want to take one further look at little words in the Bible. Prepositions are marvelous little words because they explain relationships with precision: comparison (like, as); direction (to, toward, through); location/place (in, at, by, on); possession (of); purpose (for); source (from, out of); and time (at, before, on). The Box in the title is not the TV in your lounge but an illustration of prepositions in relationship with a location, a place. Some teachers use a circle to illustrate these small words, but I prefer the visual three-dimensional box illustration.

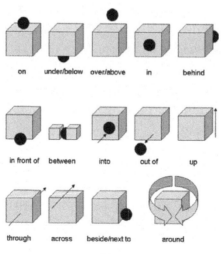

Prepositions show their relationship or their position to the Box. They can also tell us why or when something takes place or they can give us a general description. One website lists 150 prepositions in the English language, while the biblical Greek uses only around 17, nine of which depend on the grammar for their meaning. With a preposition in four out of five verses, they are everywhere in the Bible! (Again, you will need an essentially literal translation for this!)

For example, in Deuteronomy 6:23 Moses speaks about the Jewish nation and the land of Egypt: *"And he brought us out from there, that he might bring us in and give us the land that he swore to give to our fathers."* Speaking of Abraham, Stephen said in Acts 7:4, *"Then he went out from the land of the Chaldeans and lived in Haran. And after his father died, God removed him from there into this land in which you are now living."* We are able to understand these journeys in the physical world because of the precision of prepositions.

In much the same way, we can understand spiritual truths with precision. I'm urging you to believe prepositions in a spiritual context as much as you believe them in the physical world. *"Now unto him that is able to do exceeding abundantly above all that we ask or think, according to the power at work within us"* (Ephesians 3:20). When we believe it we'll start seeing the effects of the power of God at work within us; that's where the power resides, in us! It is not in the church building or the congregation but in the individual, so you have it always.

"Being freely justified by his grace, through the redemption that is in Christ Jesus" (Romans 3:24). All our blessings come by his grace, which is made available to us through the death and resurrection of Christ Jesus. *"More than that, we also rejoice in God through our Lord Jesus*

*Christ, **through** whom we have now received reconciliation"* (Romans 5:11). It's shouting time for believers! Through Christ we have much to rejoice about.

Yet another preposition is "with." It is used in Paul's letters as "with Christ," and has to do with both past and future events. *"But God... ⁵made us alive **together with** Christ — by grace you have been saved — ⁶and raised us up **with** him and seated us **with** him in the heavenly places **in** Christ Jesus"* (Ephesians 2:4-6). God did this at the resurrection with Jesus. The old spiritual song asks, "Were you there when they raised him from the dead?" And now you can answer, "Yes!", because to God, Christ and you went through that event together. It was physically true of Christ and spiritually true for you.

As to the future, Paul declared, *"My desire is to depart and be **with** Christ, for that is far better"* (Philippians 1:24). It is always an interesting paradox for the Christian, because as we talk and sing about how wonderful heaven will be, our attitude is sometimes, "Not right now, Lord, if you don't mind!" Paul went on to say, *"But to remain **in** the flesh is more necessary [**for** you] on your account"* (verse 25). So he only wanted to stay around because he could see that the believers had yet to grasp the great truths he was teaching.

Paul wrote the letter to the Galatians because of false teachers who were trying to mix the Jewish faith based on works with the Christian faith based on grace. *"Yet because of [**through**] false brothers secretly brought in — who slipped **in** to spy out our freedom that we have **in** Christ Jesus, so that they might bring us [**down**] into slavery"* (Galatians 2:4).

Galatians also gives us a powerful summary of the Christian life. *"I have been crucified **with** Christ. It is no longer I who live, but Christ who lives **in** me. And the life I* *now live in the flesh I live by faith in the Son of God, who loved me and gave himself for me"* (Galatians 2:20).

So again, I urge you to read **what is written,** and then to pause and think about the precision of God's Word to you *"Now we did not receive the spirit of the world, but the Spirit which is from God, in order that we might know the things freely given to us by God"* (II Corinthians 2:12).

15
God's Perfect Word

Some people wonder why I so strongly encourage people to read God's Word in an essentially literal translation and think about what they read. The answer is really quite simple. Since **God is perfect**, His Words, like all His works, are perfect. There is no higher authority for the Christian believer. Yet so many treat the Bible as optional and relative rather than essential and absolute.

"The law of the Lord is perfect, reviving the soul" (Psalm 19:7). *"This God — his way is perfect; the word of the Lord proves true"* (Psalm 18:30). *"Every word of God is pure"* (Proverbs 30:5 KJV). *"For no prophecy was ever produced by the will of man, but men spoke from God as they were carried along by the Holy Spirit"* (II Peter 1:21).

"We shall not be surprised therefore to find literary perfection as well as spiritual perfection" (E.W. Bullinger). God has to be the ultimate grammarian and linguist. Since we believe what the Bible itself declares, that it is "God-breathed" (II Timothy 3:16 AMP), then the order and structure will reflect this within the limits of the language to whom it was given and the limits of our own language.

Again we get back to how the original manuscripts

looked: just large paragraphs in Hebrew and in the Greek uncial manuscripts a string of characters with no spaces between words, and no numbered lists or bulleted lists or indents or any type of punctuation. So the **structure** has to be evident by the choice of words used and the order in which they were used.

For example, Isaiah 55:6 shows a correspondence, "*Seek the Lord while he may be found; Call upon him while he is near*"; the same thought but given in different terms.

Proverbs 27:6 shows a contrast, "*Faithful are the wounds of a friend, But deceitful are the kisses of an enemy*" (NASB).

When you see these, mark them in your Bible. There are only two ways in which a subject is repeated: by alternation or introversion, to use the technical terms. Another way of showing it is A, B, A, B for alternation and A, B, B, A for introversion. An example of introversion is Isaiah 6:10,

"*Make the [A] heart of this people dull, and their [B] ears heavy, and blind their [C] eyes; lest they see with their [C] eyes, and hear with their [B] ears, and understand with their [A] hearts, and turn and be healed.*"

A repetition of a word is another good indication of structure. We covered this earlier. "*... that you may know what is the hope to which he has called you, what are the riches of his glorious inheritance in the saints, and what is the immeasurable greatness of his power toward us who believe...*" (Ephesians 1:18-19). If you underline each "what" you will always see the structure of a list.

So structure helps us to discover what a passage is about, its scope or subject, and the key to its meaning. "*The works of the Lord are great, studied by all who have pleasure in them*" (Psalm 111:2 NKJV). "*God's works are so great, worth a lifetime of study — endless enjoyment!*" (MSG).

16
Tools for the Worker

"Do your best to present yourself to God as one approved, a worker who has no need to be ashamed, rightly handling the word of truth" (II Timothy 2:15). Every worker needs the right tools for the task at hand, and with the right tools enjoys creating masterpieces or restoring damages, for example. "Rightly handling" literally means "correctly cutting," so the Amplified Bible reads "correctly analyzing and accurately dividing," the Concordant Literal Version reads "correctly cutting the word of truth" and Darby's 1889 Bible, *"cutting in a straight line the word of truth."*

To conclude this more technical area, I want to suggest some tools that are lifetime investments. I will deal with books first, and then digital products. First you need an **essentially literal translation**, and there's plenty to choose from. In this category there is, in no particular order, the KJV, ASV, NASB, NKJV, HCSB and the ESV (my current preference). However, there are more tools available for the good old KJV than any other translation. I prefer a reference Bible (the references down the middle of the page and a column on either side) in a large type size so you can make your own notes above the words and in the margins.

You may prefer other popular bibles, such as the NIV, but they were created to "balance transparency to the original with clarity of meaning" (https://www.thenivbible.com), in other words combining a paraphrase with an essentially literal translation, but failing to indicate which parts are which.

For example, in II Corinthians 5:17 the NIV reads, *"The old has gone, the new has come!"* There is no change of doctrine or inaccuracy there, but they failed to translate one Greek word. Between the two phrases, God placed the word "behold" or "lo" or "see," to stop the flow and emphasize the greatness and importance of the new. So in the NIV we just notice the contrast but in most literal translations we pause and focus our thoughts on the new. So the translators have ignored Matthew 4:4 about "every word." In other places, the NIV translators have inserted their own doctrinal preferences, and you can check the internet for discussions on this.

In many of the verses I have already quoted you cannot see the truth in a paraphrased version. Such Bibles are good sources for illustrative phrases, and in a recent book I quoted from over 15 other Bible versions and paraphrases in addition to the ESV, so I make good use of them in my teaching.

An *annotated Bible* is a standard bible with marginal references and comments on words to save you looking up an outside source. Some use symbols in the text, or footnotes and appendices, to give you textual help. Examples would be the Companion Bible, the Thompson Chain Reference Bible, or the older Newberry Bible; all three are KJV based. A.E. Knoch, who produced the Concordant Literal Version (download sample chapters at http://www.concordant.org/version/clntsamp.pdf/) wore out two Newberry Bibles and a Wigram's Concordance in his studies!

On the other hand, a *study Bible* is influenced more by

the beliefs of the producers, with doctrinal teaching in addition to marginal references. The original Scofield Study Bible (KJV), Dake's Annotated Reference Bible (KJV), ESV Study Bible, New Spirit-Filled Life Bible, and scores of other study bibles are on the market.

Second on the list is a *concordance*, a valuable aid that lists usages of a word. You can download our list of "In Christ" scriptures at www.peterwade.com/wp-content/uploads/in-christ-letter.pdf, which is really a concordance of that phrase. Popular choices of concordances are Strong's and Young's and Cruden's; huge volumes with every one of the 12,143 words in the King James Version. The first two also give the meaning of Hebrew and Greek words.

Other concise concordances are available; some small concordances are even bound with various translations. If you remember part of a verse and want to read the whole or the context, this is the tool you use to find it. Everyone needs a concordance.

A *lexicon* is a book much like an English dictionary, which explains what a word means and how it is used. Thayer's is a long-standing favorite, as is the popular *Vine's Expository Dictionary of New Testament Words*.

On the other hand, a *Bible dictionary*, like Smith's, Unger's, Holman's and many others, is actually more like an abbreviated Bible encyclopedia, describing places, people, flora and fauna, currency, measurements, and so forth.

Turning to the *digital world*, many of the long established books mentioned above are available online at sites such as www.bible.org and www.biblestudytools.com and many others. Better yet,many Bible programs are available for different operating systems, ranging from free to $100 and up. These combine all the above in one program or linked programs, and are widely used.

For those with a Windows or Mac operating systems plus iPhone and iPad, you shouldn't pass up *E-Sword* from www.e-sword.net, which is what I personally use. E-Sword is free, so you can't beat the price! It combines all the above types of books, with multiple translations, resources, and even your own note-taking area. See the screenshots on their home page. There have been 30 million downloads to date! You can purchase additional recent Bibles to add to the stack you get with your free download.

So I encourage you to get your Word Toolbox organized and use it to enjoy your Bible even more!

17
"I'll make every word I give you come true."

The integrity of God's Word is everything. It is the number one problem people have. By this I mean God is either to be believed or it matters little what else is debated about Him. I'm not alone is this belief. I did a search on Google for "integrity of God's word" and I was presented with over two million results! Of course, some of comments found may have been opposed to it but a quick glance indicates that most believe in it.

So how does it work out in our daily lives? If you were taught in college that the Bible was just a collection of myths and fables, and you bought into that idea, it doesn't change the integrity of God's Word. It has integrity whether you believe it or not. But your lack of acceptance will mean God's promises will not work in your life. Name any problem you have right now, and its answer is you need to work on your understanding of the integrity of the Word.

*"Know this: God, your God, is God indeed, **a God you can depend upon**. He keeps his covenant of loyal love with those who love him and observe his commandments for a thousand generations"* (Deuteronomy 7:9 MSG).

*"Blessed be the Lord who has given rest to his people Israel, according to all that he promised. **Not one word has failed** of all his good promise, which he spoke by Moses his servant"* (I Kings 8:56 ESV).

To Jeremiah, God said *"I'll make every word I give you come true"* (Jeremiah 1:12 MSG).

And we could fill this book with similar statements from both testaments of the Bible. God's Word has integrity. Accept it, believe it, confess it—and enjoy it!

Appendix
Figures of Speech–An Introduction

For those who want to "dig a little deeper"

God has declared that *"All Scripture is breathed out by God and profitable for teaching, for reproof, for correction, and for training in righteousness, that the man of God may be competent, equipped for every good work"* (II Timothy 3:16,17 ESV). Since we are dealing with the God-breathed Word, we should be very careful to apply logically and accurately the rules of grammar and language.

One major area that is so often overlooked or misunderstood is the field of figures of speech. Unfortunately many sincere believers, when confronted with a statement in the Bible that is obviously not true to fact, declare, "Oh, that's only figurative," as if it were of little importance. Their understanding of what God is saying would come alive for them if they only realized that the reverse is true — it is not "only figurative" but that part of the Word that the Father wishes to emphasize.

Figures of speech are legitimate departures from accepted grammatical forms in order to give emphasis and emotion to what has been written or spoken. In the Word of God, figures of speech are God's marking as to what is important. When

God gave the New Testament epistles to holy men, they committed it to writing in uncial letters — what we would term capital or upper-case letters. There were no breaks between words and no punctuation. For example, the first part of John 3:16 would look like this (in English): FORGODSOLOVEDTHEWORLDTHATHEGAVE...

Today printers and publishers have many mechanical devices available to them when they wish to emphasize a word or a phrase. The word can be set in *italic type* (a typeface that slopes to the right), or in **bold face type** (a heavy black typeface), or it can be set in all CAPITAL letters or underlined. Using any of these methods, the word will stand out clearly from the rest of the text. Also, with the right use of punctuation, a writer can show the reader what he feels is the impact of the sentence. There are various rules that govern these matters, rules that vary from language to language.

Mechanical methods of marking have changed down through the years, yet for God's Word to be accurate and applicable to all generations in all nations, some perfect method of emphasis was needed. God, in His great wisdom, employed figures of speech as the timeless and accurate way in which to give His emphasis, to His life-giving Word.

It may be true for several reasons that we may not immediately understand the figure that is employed, but we should endeavor to recognize that a figure of speech is before us. Then our task is that of II Timothy 2:15: *"Do your best to present yourself to God as one approved, a worker who has no need to be ashamed, rightly handling the word of truth."* Workers need tools, and this introductory discussion of figures of speech is designed to open your mind to the presence and meaning of some of the major figures, and thus bring you closer to the mind of God as He revealed Himself in the Word.

The major Christian work in this field is *Figures of Speech Used in the Bible* by E. W Bullinger (first published in 1898 and still in print), a monumental 1,100-page treatise explaining and illustrating some 212 figures of speech the author had recognized in the Word of God. (You can read extracts from the Introduction online as an article on our site: www.peterwade.com/articles/bullinger/ground-is-thirsty . I am acquainted with only one other work that discusses figures of speech in any detail, and that is a 40-page appendix to the *Keyword Concordance to the New Testament* (Concordant Publishing Concern, 1970 edition; sadly omitted from current editions but available on my website with their permission as an article by A.E. Knoch: www.peterwade.com/articles/other/figures-of-speech). This appendix is especially recommended, for it is designed for those who do not know the Biblical languages nor the technical terms for the various figures. What follows is largely based on these two works.

In the introductory paragraph to the appendix mentioned above, the unnamed author (possibly A.E. Knoch) sets the stage beautifully with these words: "God, Who studded the sky with jewels and carpeted the earth with colors, has written His revelation in language which reflects the beauties of His visible creation. The diction of the East and of the Scriptures is full of fine figures, over which we walk with ruthless tread, seldom stopping to admire the blooms beneath our feet. It is the voice of feeling as well as fact. Nor is its beauty merely ornamental. Unless our eyes are opened to their presence and we feel their force, we may fail to enter beneath the surface of bare facts, into the heart of God's truth, and be led astray by mere externals."

How to Recognize a Figure of Speech

Dr. E. W. Bullinger introduces his great work with these

helpful words: "A figure is simply a word or a sentence thrown into peculiar *form,* different from its original or simplest meaning or use. These forms are constantly used by every speaker or writer. It is impossible to hold the simplest conversation, or to write a few sentences without, it may be unconsciously, making use of figures. We may say, 'the ground needs rain': that is a plain, cold, matter-of-fact statement; but if we say 'the ground is thirsty', we immediately use a figure. It is not true to *fact* as soil cannot drink, and therefore it must be a figure. But how true to *feeling* it is! How full of warmth and life! Hence we say, 'the crops suffer'; we speak of 'a hard heart,' 'a rough man,' 'an iron will.' In all these cases we take a word which has a certain, definite meaning, and apply the name, or the quality, or the act, to some other thing with which it is associated, by time or place, cause or effect, relation or resemblance.

"It may be asked, 'How are we to know, then, when words are to be taken in their simple, original form (i.e. literally), and when they are to be taken in some other and peculiar form (i.e. as a figure)?' The answer is that, whenever and wherever it is possible, the words of Scripture are to be understood *literally,* but when a statement appears to be contrary to our experience, or to known fact, or revealed truth, or seems to be at variance with the general teaching of the Scriptures, then we may reasonably expect that some figure is employed. And as it is employed only to call our attention to some specially designed emphasis, we are at once bound to diligently examine the figure for the purpose of discovering and learning the truth that is thus emphasized.

"There is an additional reason for using greater exactitude and care when we are dealing with the words of God. Man's words are scarcely worthy of such study. Man uses figures, but often at random and often in ignorance or in error. But *'the words of the Lord are pure words'* (Psalm 12:6). All His works are perfect, and when the Holy Spirit takes up and uses human words, He does so, we may be sure, with unerring accuracy, infinite wisdom, and perfect beauty. We may well, therefore, give all our attention to *'words not taught by human wisdom but taught by the Spirit'* (I Corinthians 2:13)." Thus, with great clarity and beauty, Bullinger introduces the subject.

It may come as a shock to you to realize that much of God's Word is not *literally* true. Some of its most precious and important statements simply cannot be taken as they stand. This is perhaps as great a shock as that when you first discovered that the Bible was an Eastern book and that the customs and mannerisms you were reading about have little in common with the way a Westerner lives today. Neither of these concepts are contradictory to the great truth of the God-inspired Word. They are just an acknowledgement of the *way* in which God handled human words as a vehicle of His thoughts and of the *cultural* background against which His words are set.

When Jesus told his disciples *"Our friend Lazarus has fallen asleep, but I go to awaken him,"* they took His words literally and were thus mistaken. The words spoken by Jesus were not false, they were figurative. *"Then Jesus told them plainly, 'Lazarus has died'"* (see John 11:11-14). Some of the greatest statements found in the Word of God are emphasized and shown their importance by the use of a figure. Anything in God's Word that is not literally true to fact is not false, it is figurative. When God spoke, He said what He meant, and it is up to us to show ourselves as *"a worker who has no need to be ashamed."*

Classifying the figures

The Greeks and the Romans devised several ways in which figures of speech can be classified. Most of these are too involved and somewhat unnecessary to our present discussion. Perhaps it is sufficient to say that all figures can be classified under the following major heads:

1. Figures involving omission;

2. Figures involving addition; and

3. Figures involving change.

This classification does throw some light on the fact of how figures are produced from plain statements of fact. Some figures deliberately leave out words in order to hurry the reader on to the important part of the statement; other figures add words in order to slow the reader down; and yet other figures change words or change the order of words in order to catch the reader's attention.

In the time of Shakespeare and the time of the King James Bible, every grammar school student would have been able to recognize the figures we will be discussing, and also give to them their correct Greek or Latin name (see *Shakespeare's Use of the Arts of Language* by Miriam Joseph [Part One]; 1947). What ground we have lost in these days of "enlightenment"! To help you remember the figures of speech that I will discuss and illustrate, I am going to use English names for them (as given in the Keyword Concordance) and not the technical names. Should you wish to know the technical names, I suggest you obtain or access Bullinger's work.

I believe it will take a lifetime of study to know and recognize the vast number of figures in God's Word. However, the important thing at this point of time is for you to start recognizing one or two, so that when you do, you will stop your reading and think: "Now, what is God emphasizing here?" The more often you observe a figure, the more you will recognize it the next time and thus grow in your appreciation of its greatness.

Literal and figurative meanings

There is a great problem in not distinguishing between the literal and the figurative meanings of words. This has caused tremendous confusion with commentators and with lexicons and concordances. Too often a figurative usage has been taken and listed as an alternative meaning of a word. Then someone comes along, checks out the listing, and picks the meaning that suits their particular theology or thinking on the subject at hand. That word may have been used in a figurative sense in one part of the Bible, but that does not mean that it can be applied somewhere else to suit the students work or theology. This is a problem in translations such as the Amplified Bible.

"In seeking to fix the exact significance of a word, only its literal usage should be consulted. Here alone the actual meaning appears. The figurative is a departure from it" (*Keyword Concordance*, pp. 350-351). There is a definite principle that should be constantly in mind: "The literal meaning of a word is one and constant; the figurative usage is diverse and variable" (p. 351).

The basic meaning of a word will remain the same, and its figurative meaning will still bear some resemblance to the basic meaning. Let us also remember that as we attempt to establish the variation in the figurative meaning, we must always go back first to the basic meaning and work out from there. Do not take a figurative meaning and allow it to influence your understanding of the basic meaning, for if the foundation is not sure, the superstructure will tumble.

Let us also beware of applying a figurative meaning to all

usages of one word. For example, even though in one parable we are told that *"the sower sows the word"* (Mark 4:14), we cannot assume that every time the word "seed" or "sowing" is mentioned that it refers to the Word of God. In another parable the *"good seed is the sons of the kingdom"* (Matthew 13:38). Let us only apply a figure where it belongs.

Since figures of speech are the Holy Spirit's markings as to what is important in the Word, it will become an interesting and vital subject for every believer that is really concerned about what God has spoken to them. Do we need any other motive for our study?

Figures of likeness

Figures of likeness are employed where there is a comparison to be considered. The important fact about figures of likeness is that they depend on unlikeness. The two objects being compared must be unlike in the main yet similar in perhaps one or more particulars in order to be a figure. Under no circumstance must the likeness be allowed to go beyond these particulars or the figure is violated. This rule is often broken by the enthusiasm of some preachers when dealing with the many parables in the Word. A parable is a figure of likeness, yet the likeness is only to be considered in the salient points and not in the multitude of detail that is given in order to make the word picture complete.

I will illustrate the problem with an example from the Book of Revelation. It matters little to endeavour to assign a meaning to a hair on the end of one of the ten horns of the seven-headed beast that rose out of the sea (Revelation 13:1). That the beast itself is symbolic of someone or something is obvious, but the majority of the detail is given to complete the picture, so that the symbol is not confused with other beasts or persons in the Book of Revelation who also have horns.

Figures of Resemblance

All figures of likeness may be expanded into a simile by adding the formula "is like." This is a simple test to determine whether the figure is to be recognized as a figure of likeness. A simile actually states that one thing is like or similar to another in some respect—*"All flesh is like grass (I Peter 1:24)."* The metaphor is bolder, for it leaves the realm of fact and says that one thing is another—*"All flesh is grass."*

Now let us think about these two statements for a moment. In what way are human beings *like* grass? At first thought you would say there is very little agreement between a blade of grass and a fine example of humanity like yourself. But God has used the expression "all flesh is like grass" and there must be a reason for such an emphasis to be made. By using such a figure, God is showing that there is some really tremendous truth to be understood.

I Peter 1:24-25 actually makes the statement we have been considering. Sometimes in the translation of the Word of God, the word "as" is used where in other places the word "like" is found, and whenever you see either word you should stop and consider whether the figure of resemblance (simile) is present. Now let us read the verse and endeavour to discover what resemblance there is between a blade of grass and humanity. *"For all flesh is like grass and all its glory like the flower of grass. The grass withers, and the flower falls, but the word of the Lord remains forever."*

The immediate context indicates that the resemblance is in the area of the life span of grass. Grass grows quickly, and in time of drought dries up quickly. When compared to the eternal endurance of God's Word, the life span of man is seen to be as short as that of grass. Obviously we should give more time to those things that last for ever, than to those short-lived material things that we think are such an important part of our life.

Now we can see the beauty of the figure of resemblance. It is a figure because it is not true to fact. I see people every day of my life and yet I have not seen anyone yet that looks like a blade of grass! I have seen some who are thinner than I am, with only room for one stripe down their pyjama pants, but they are still not like a blade of grass! And so the statement before us is a figure, and it is the figure of resemblance, for God has pointed to some resemblance between grass and humanity.

So that we understand this particular figure better, I want to take a further example of its use, this time from Psalm 1. As we read verse 3 you will notice the word "like" is employed: *"He is like a tree planted by streams of water that yields its fruit in its season, and its leaf does not wither. In all that he does, he prospers."* The word "he" refers back to the man described in verse 2, and the figure of resemblance is used to emphasize some resemblance between this man and a tree. It is obviously a figure for we have yet to see a man who actually looks like a tree. Now the righteous man is compared, not with any tree, but with one that is receiving adequate moisture for growth (in this particular case, by irrigation), one that bears its fruit at the right season, and one that shows its continual life by the luxuriant canopy of green leaves. What a beautiful tree, standing there in all its glory! And each point of resemblance mentioned has a parallel in the life of a righteous man, who has all the potential for fruit-bearing and prosperity as does the tree.

Verse 4 declares that *"the wicked are not so."* None of the glorious aspects of the life of the righteous man are found in the ungodly. Verse 4 continues: *"... but are like chaff that the wind drives away."* The old method of separating the chaff from the wheat was to throw the wheat into the air on a windy day. The chaff would be blown to one side while the wheat would fall down into the dish again. "The wicked... are like the chaff." They serve no useful purpose, but are only fit to be blown away, separated from the prosperous godly people. The figure is again that of resemblance.

Now the same truth could be stated very plainly without the use of a figure in perhaps this way: "The righteous are stable, prosperous people but the wicked are useless people." But how that lacks color and feeling! How much better is the tremendous picture we see in our minds of luxuriant trees lining an irrigation channel versus dried-up chaff carried by the wind. Can you now see the beauty and impact of figures of speech? God has carefully placed His emphasis in the Word and our observation of it brings much blessing.

Let us now look at a parable in our quest for an understanding of the figure of resemblance. You will no doubt remember the two houses, one built upon a rock and the other built upon sand. Matthew 7:24-27 contains the record. *"Everyone then who hears these words of mine and does them will be like* [there is the word "like" and it indicates that the figure of resemblance is now going to be employed] *a wise man who built his house on the rock. ²⁵And the rain fell, and the floods came, and the winds blew and beat on that house, but it did not fall, because it had been founded on the rock."* The picture is vivid, isn't it? It is an illustration of a person who hears the word of God and who applies it by action to his or her life. This one is standing firm on the solid foundation of the Word, even though the storms of limiting appearances and unbelief are raging around.

"²⁶And everyone who hears these words of mine and does

not do them will be like [the word "like" again, indicating the figure of resemblance] *a foolish man who built his house on the sand. ²⁷And the rain fell, and the floods came, and the winds blew and beat against that house, and it fell, and great was the fall of it."* Again the picture is so vivid that is leaves very little to the imagination. In fact, for added emphasis the two pictures are set in perfect contrast one to the other. The one hearing and walking on the Word of God is contrasted with the one who is not. The house built upon the rock is contrasted with that on the sand. The steadfastness of one is contrasted with the insecurity of the other. The language is figurative but it is not false; it is loaded with emphasis and vitality so that we comprehend the truth that God's Word is teaching in these verses.

One further example of resemblance will have to suffice. Isaiah 24:2-3 makes this statement: *"And it shall be, as with the people, so with the priest; as with the slave, so with his master; as with the maid, so with her mistress; as with the buyer, so with the seller; as with the lender, so with the borrower; as with the creditor, so with the debtor. ³The earth shall be utterly empty and utterly plundered; for the Lord has spoken this word."*

The words "as" and "so" also indicate that the figure is that of resemblance, and you will notice that they are used six times in verse 2. The emphasis is made strongly that absolutely everybody in the land was going to be affected by this situation. For example, there are lots of differences between a servant and his master, and yet here they have one point of likeness — they will both be affected by the judgement of God. The emphasis is so strong as you read down through verse 2 that by the time you get to the end of the verse you are really wondering what is going to happen to all these people, and the climax comes in verse 3 when you discover that the land is going to be emptied and plundered.

Figures of Representation

You will recall that we illustrated the previous figure of resemblance by the phrase *"all flesh is like grass."* Now we take the thought one step deeper by the figure of representation and say *"all flesh is grass."* This gives much greater impact and makes the comparison bolder. The figure is correctly known as a metaphor, a Greek word meaning a transference or a carrying over. However, the word "metaphor" and the phrase "metaphorically speaking" are so commonly used in English to designate any or all figures of speech, that I suggest you do not use it as a label for the figure of representation.

Having defined the term, notice Isaiah 40:6-7: *"A voice says, 'Cry!' And I said, 'What shall I cry?' All flesh is grass, and all its beauty is like the flower of the field... ⁷surely the people are grass..."* The emphasis is made bolder by declaring that one thing is another. To give further examples, *"All we like sheep..."* (Isaiah 53:6) is the figure of resemblance; *"We are... the sheep of his pasture ..."* (Psalm 100:3) is the figure of representation.

Perhaps it will help if I give this illustration. Suppose I take a photograph out of my wallet and show it to you. I might say, "This is me ten years ago." But that is a figure of speech, for it is not true to fact that a little piece of shiny paper is actually me! However, the image on the paper is a representation of me, and it depends on the ability of the photographer as to whether it is a good or a bad representation! Now you might think (and with good cause) that I was being pedantic if I said, "This is a representation of me recorded by photography ten years ago!" But since English-speaking persons prefer to omit words rather than add them, we constantly use the figure of representation, and would say, "This is me ten years ago."

"You are the salt of the earth..." (Matthew 5:13). You represent to the world what salt represents to other things — preservation from corruption. *"I am the door.."* (John 10:9). Christ represents the function of a door. Christ is the entrance to the sheepfold and to the Father. In both these examples you will notice that there is "a distinct affirmation that one thing is another thing, owing to some association or connection in the uses or effects of anything expressed or understood" (Bullinger). It could be said that the figure of representation is an abbreviated figure of resemblance, for it omits the statement of likeness.

We see a further example of the figure of representation in Matthew 13:36-39. Jesus had taught the multitude a number of parables, and then He sent them away. He went into a house, *"And his disciples came to him, saying, 'Explain to us the parable of the weeds of the field.' 37He answered, 'The one who sows the good seed is the Son of Man.'"*

The one who is sowing the seed in the parable represents our Lord Jesus Christ. It was not Jesus himself who was sowing the seed in the field, for it is only a parable, a figure of representation. *"38The field is the world"*; no, it is not— one field is not the whole world. So the phrase is not true to fact, therefore it must be a figure of speech. The word "is" indicates that one thing is said to be another, and so it is a representation—the field represents the world.

"The good seed is the children of the kingdom"; the seed represents them. *"The weeds are* [represent] *the the sons of*

the evil one; [39]*the enemy that sowed them is [represents] the devil; the harvest is* [represents] *the close of the age; and the reapers are* [represent] *angels.*" The figure of representation is used in a series to interpret the parable. Every major part of that parable has some meaning, but in order to make it clear to us a figure had to be employed, the figure of representation.

Now let us examine a statement of fact in John 4:24. This is part of the discussion Jesus had with the woman of Samaria at the well. Jesus said to her, *"God is spirit, and those who worship him must worship in spirit and truth."* The present form of the verb "to be" ["is"] is not present in the Greek but is necessary in English, and so it appears in italics in the KJV. The italics indicate what has been added by the translators. However, the absence of the verb "to be" in the Greek is proof that the phrase "God a spirit" is not a figure but absolute truth. In fact, the text reads "Spirit *is* God," placing the emphasis upon the nature of God as a truth to be comprehended.

Now keep that truth in mind as we look at the I John 4:8, where we read another statement concerning God. *"He that loveth not knoweth not God; for God is love."* The word "is" is present in the original text and here we have a figure of representation, because the plain statement of fact in John 4:24 was that "God *is* Spirit." Now we read that "God is love." Everything about God speaks of love, God acts on the basis of love, God sheds abroad His love, God is the ultimate picture of love, but actually "God *is* Spirit." John 4:24 is literally true, but I John 4:8 is a figure.

We have then a beautiful figure emphasizing that one of God's characteristics is love. You could read many other statements in the Word that declare God is light, God is holy, God is pure, God is just, and you will find all these have the verb "to be" in the statement and are therefore representations.

These figures of speech emphasize and bring to our attention some part of God's character. If you will read the rest of the discussion in I John chapter 4, you will find that from verse 7 onwards it concerns love down through to verse 12, and then from verse 16 to verse 21. The whole context has to do with love, and so through a figure of speech God's attribute of love is emphasized to us. There would be very little virtue in saying throughout that passage that God *is* Spirit, but to show one of His characteristics, that God is [represents] love, has tremendous impact in the whole argument.

One characteristic of God is love, and since we are children of God we ought to be expressing the same kind of love that God has. How tremendous it is to recognise the figure of representation in the Word of God. It is most important in the New Testament to observe whether the verb "to be" is present or not, and to do this you may need to check a version such as the Concordant Literal New Testament, Newberry's Bible, The Companion Bible, or some other annotated Bible that will indicate this to you.

Figures of Implication

Let us take our study one step further and observe the figure of implication. Perhaps this is the most frequently employed figure of speech in the Word of God. In the figure of resemblance which we have already discussed, we would perhaps say, "You are like a beast." In the figure of representation, we might say to somebody, "You are a beast", but when we come to the figure of implication, we would simply say to that person "Beast!" The figure of implication does not have any likeness in it, as does resemblance, and it does not need a verb; it simply comes straight to the point and the implication is inherent—"Beast!"

Here are some examples of this figure. In Matthew 16:6,

we read of the teaching of Jesus: *"Jesus said to them, 'Watch and beware of the leaven of the Pharisees and Sadducees.'"* Leaven is like the yeast that you put into the dough of bread so that it rises. Leaven is a physical thing. Now surely Jesus is not talking about the ability of the Pharisees and the Sadducees to make bread. No, it must be a figurative usage, the figure of implication.

That the disciples were not well trained in figures of speech is clear from verse 7: *"And they began discussing it among themselves, saying, 'We brought no bread.'"* They took the figure literally! *"⁸But Jesus, aware of this, said, "O you of little faith, why are you discussing among yourselves the fact that you have no bread? ⁹Do you not yet perceive? Do you not remember the five loaves for the five thousand, and how many baskets you gathered? ¹⁰Or the seven loaves for the four thousand, and how many baskets you gathered? ¹¹How is it that you fail to understand that I did not speak about bread? Beware of the leaven of the Pharisees and Sadducees. ¹²Then they understood that he did not tell them to beware of the leaven of bread, but of the teaching of the Pharisees and Sadducees"* (verses 8-12). Isn't that a tremendous record?

Now that is where most Christian believers sit today; they just do not realise the figures that are employed. The disciples should have known that when Jesus spoke of the leaven of the Pharisees and the Sadducees, he was not talking about buying bread from that group, for bread is not related to Pharisees and Sadducees; they were not known as bakers in the community. They were sects within the Jewish faith, and each of those names, Pharisees and Sadducees, represented a particular viewpoint within the Jewish religion. Why relate bread to religion? It doesn't fit, so we have a figure, and the figure is implication. I believe that perhaps this incident is one of the best illustrations on record of the need to understand figures of speech in the Word of God.

Here's another example from Matthew 15:22-27. Jesus had come to the coast, into the area of Tyre and Sidon, *"And behold, a Canaanite woman from that region came out and was crying, 'Have mercy on me, O Lord, Son of David; my daughter is severely oppressed by a demon.' 23But he did not answer her a word. And his disciples came and begged him, saying, 'Send her away, for she is crying out after us.' 24He answered, 'I was sent only to the lost sheep of the house of Israel.' 25But she came and knelt before him, saying, 'Lord, help me.' 26And he answered, 'It is not right to take the children's bread and throw it to the dogs'"* (verses 22-26).

Now wait a minute, we have read nothing prior to this about dogs. Why are dogs suddenly brought into the discussion? Because it is a figure of speech, a figure of implication. This woman from Canaan was not part of the Jewish religion and this was why Jesus said that He came only to the lost house of Israel, the Jewish people. He said that you do not take bread that belongs to the children and cast it to the dogs. You do not take the help that is intended for the Jewish people and give it to the other nations. Therefore, by implication, the word "dogs" is used for people who are outside the Jewish faith. But this woman turned it around beautifully and in verse 27 she said, *"She said, 'Yes, Lord, yet even the dogs eat the crumbs that fall from their masters' table'."* And she received what she wanted through the grace of Jesus.

This same figure of implication is used in Psalm 22:16, a prophecy concerning Jesus on the cross, and it says that *"for dogs encompass me."* Now this was written not to indicate that there were many dogs running around the foot of the cross, but by implication the fact that at the time of his death

Gentiles would be surrounding the cross.

Let us look at another example of implication, this time in John 2:18-21: *"So the Jews said to him, 'What sign do you show us for doing these things?' [19]Jesus answered them, 'Destroy this temple, and in three days I will raise it up.' [20]The Jews then said, 'It has taken forty-six years to build this temple, and will you raise it up in three days?' [21]But he was speaking about the temple of his body."* Once again a figure of speech was misunderstood by the hearers. By implication Jesus said, "Destroy this temple, that is, my body, and in three days I will raise it up." Instead of giving a lengthy dissertation on how a temple and a body have certain similarities between them, the temple is simply substituted for the body, and we have the figure of implication.

For a final example, notice Acts 20:29: *"I know that after my departure fierce wolves will come in among you, not sparing the flock."* Is it true to fact? No, Paul was not concerned that there were wolves coming to church. It is a figure, a figure of implication concerning those who would come in and spoil the church in the same way as wolves would spoil a flock of sheep. So instead of saying that people with wolf-like characteristics are going to come into this group of believers, he said, by implication, "Wolves will enter in among you and spoil the flock."

This figure is used constantly throughout the Word of God. It is a bold figure, a strong figure, but in order to recognize it you must have your thinking abilities in full working order. Implication is one of the figures of likeness.

Parable

A parable is simply an extended figure of likeness in the form of a story—a likeness with action. It is "a story with a hidden meaning, without pressing in every detail, the idea of a comparison… This likeness is generally only in some special point. One person may be like another in appearance, but not in character, and vice versa; so that when resemblance or likeness is affirmed it is not to be concluded that the likeness may be pressed in all points, or extended to all particulars. For example, a lion is used as a resemblance of Christ, on account of his strength and prowess. The devil is likened to a lion because of violence and cruelty. Christ is compared to a thief, on account of his coming being unexpected; not on account of dishonesty" (Bullinger).

In Luke 4:23 we have the shortest named parable in the Word of God. *"And he said to them, 'Doubtless you will quote to me this proverb, "Physician, heal yourself"'"* (The Greek text actually reads "parable," this being the only place the KJV translators have rendered *parabole* as "proverb.") Jesus is compared to a physician who attends on his own case, and the action of a physician is added to the likeness. This is a beautiful parable, full of deep meaning in the likeness suggested and the action—the physician should cure himself.

Another parable is found in Matthew 13:24-30: *"He put another parable before them, saying, 'The kingdom of heaven may be compared to a man who sowed good seed in his field, [25]but while his men were sleeping, his enemy came and sowed weeds among the wheat and went away. [26]So when the plants came up and bore grain, then the weeds appeared also. [27]And the servants of the master of the house came and said to him, "Master, did you not sow good seed in your field? How then does it have weeds?" [28]He said to them, "An enemy has done this." So the servants said to him, "Then do you want us to go and gather them?" [29]But he said, "No, lest in gathering the weeds you root up the wheat along with them. [30]Let both grow together until the harvest, and at harvest time I will tell the reapers, 'Gather the weeds first and bind them in bundles to be burned, but gather the wheat into my barn'".*"

This parable gives much detail and it is necessary to establish which points have teaching value, that is, which physical things have likeness to spiritual matters and which points are merely background detail to complete the picture. Fortunately, God in His wisdom has given us the key to many of the parables, in this instance in verses 36-43 of the same chapter. The field, the good seed, the weeds, the enemy, the harvest, the reapers, and the gathering and burning of the tares, are all given a spiritual meaning. No mention is made of the men who slept (the servants of the householder), the binding into bundles of the tares, nor of the barn, and so these points are given in the story simply to complete the picture. Any attempt to allot to them spiritual significance would be to go beyond the revealed will of God.

"Perhaps the most extensive parable in the Scriptures is the tabernacle and its ritual" (Keyword Concordance). Notice Hebrews 9:8-9: *"By this the Holy Spirit indicates that the way into the holy places is not yet opened as long as the first section is still standing ⁹(which is symbolic* [the text is "parable"] *for the present age)."* A parable is simply a story giving a likeness, and by observing that likeness we can learn great spiritual truths.

I trust this introduction to figures of speech has opened your mind to see how carefully and specifically God chose the words to use when *"holy men of God spake as they were moved by the Holy Ghost"* (II Peter 1:21). *"...men spoke from God who were borne along (moved and impelled) by the Holy Spirit"* (AMP). Therefore, may you *"Study to present yourself approved to God, a workman that needs not to be ashamed, rightly dividing the word of truth"* (II Timothy 2:15).

Bible Acknowledgements

Scripture quotations marked AMP are from the Amplified® Bible, Copyright © 1954, 1958, 1962, 1964, 1965, 1987 by The Lockman Foundation. Used by permission.

Scripture quotations marked ESV are taken from The Holy Bible, English Standard Version® (ESV®). Copyright © 2007 by Crossway, a publishing ministry of Good News Publishers. Used by permission. All rights reserved.

Scripture quotations marked CLV are from the Concordant Literal New Testament, Copyright © 1976 by Concordant Publishing Concern. Used by permission.

Scripture quotations marked MSG are from The Message, Copyright © 2002, by Eugene H. Peterson. Used by permission of NavPress Publishing Group.

Scripture quotations marked NASB are from the New American Standard Version. Copyright © 1977 by The Lockman Foundation. Used by permission.

Bible Abbreviations Used

AMP Amplified Bible

ASV American Standard Version

CLV Concordant Literal Version

ESV English Standard Version

HCSB Holman Christian Standard Bible

KJV King James Version

MSG The Message

NASB New American Standard Bible

NIV New International Version

NKJV New King James Version

About the Author

PETER AND VIVIEN WADE have ministered together since 1958 and continue to do so decades later. After graduating from Bible College together, they served pastorates in Australia, and for the past 50 years have fulfilled a Bible teaching ministry in the United States and Australia, and worldwide on the Internet since 1995 (www.PeterWade.com). Peter is the author of many books and audio and video teachings, and Vivien is the author of two books of poems.

Peter and Vivien are the founders of Positive Word Ministries Inc., a trans-denominational teaching ministry, and Peter is the president. They make their home in metropolitan Adelaide, South Australia.

PETER WADE

I'm Excited About
EPHESIANS

SEATED IN THE HEAVENLIES

Ephesians: Its Structure

Most writers point out a basic division between the first three and the last three chapters of this epistle. Chapters 1, 2 and 3 primarily deal with teaching, and chapters 4, 5 and 6 with putting into practice what has been taught in the first three chapters. Along with many others, I prefer to divide the practical section into two parts, giving a three-fold division of the epistle.

To quote the headings of others, we see our: Heavenly Calling, in chapters 1, 2 and 3; Earthly Conduct, in chapter 4:1 to chapter 6:9; Satanic Conflict, in chapter 6:10-24.

Ruth Paxson divides Ephesians into: The Wealth of the Christian; The Walk of the Christian; The Warfare of the Christian. Another writer speaks of the: Christian in Christ; Christ in the Christian; Christ and the Christian versus Satan.

F.E. Marsh uses a six-fold division: The Divine Purpose (1:3-14), The Divine Power (1:15-2:22), The Divine Proclamation (3:1-13), The Divine Presence (3:14-21), The Divine Provision (4:1-16), The Divine Pattern (4:17-6:9), The Divine Panoply (6:10-20).

My personal preference is to follow Watchman Nee's three-fold division from his book *Sit, Walk, Stand.* In chapters 1, 2 and 3 the keyword is "**Sit**"—the Christian is to see himself or herself as already seated with Christ. In chapter 4:1 to chapter 6:9, the keyword is "**Walk**"—the daily life of Christ in the Christian. In chapter 6 verses 10 to 24, the keyword is "**Stand**"—the believer is taking a stand against an already defeated foe.

The order is logical. We must learn what it means to be seated with Christ before we can fully succeed in our walk, and then we can effectively take a stand against the enemy. Christianity begins with a big "Done," and we are to sit and rest in the certainty of what has been done by God through Christ. On the other hand, walking implies effort, but it is effort emanating from a place of rest, not an effort to get to a place of rest!

It is right here that most Christians demonstrate their confusion. Philippians 2:12 teaches us to *"work out your own salvation"* that is, working from the inside to the outer, *"For it is God who works in you"* (verse 13 ESV). Yet it seems that the bulk of Christian activity is to help Christians do the opposite—to work on the outer to improve the inner.

Ephesians: The Three Keywords

The keyword "Sit" or "Seated" is first seen in chapter 1, *"And what is the exceeding greatness of his power toward us who believe, according to the working of his mighty power, [20]which he worked in Christ, when he raised him from the dead, and seated him at his own right hand in the heavenly places"* (verses 19, 20). How appropriate that the first usage concerns Christ and not man! Without Christ, we are nothing. In the same way as the "rest" of Genesis 2:2,3 indicates the completion of God's creative work, so the seating of Christ in the heavenly realms indicates the completion of God's creative work in the making of a new species—the Christian.

A second usage of the keyword "Sit" or "Seated" is seen in chapter 2, *"And has raised us up together, and made us sit together in heavenly places in Christ Jesus"* (verse 6). Here we see how our history is now tied up with his-story. God no longer sees the old Peter Wade, but only the Peter Wade expression of Christ. That's exciting and powerful!

The keyword "Walk" is introduced right at the start of chapter 4, *"I therefore, a prisoner for the Lord, urge you to walk... worthy of the calling to which you were called"* (verse 1 ESV). The word "walk" literally means to "walk around" and hence "to order one's behavior," and is used eight times in Ephesians. Some translations use terms such as "to live a life" or "to live and act." First we see that our walk is to be comparable to our calling as sons and daughters of God.

Next, we are given an exhortation from a negative illustration, *"This I say therefore, and testify in the Lord, that you no longer walk as the Gentiles walk, in the vanity of their mind"* (4:17). There is to be an observable difference between our walk and that of non-Christians, as you now have Christ within. Interestingly, the first item on the list concerns how our thinking relates to our walk.

In chapter 5 we are encouraged to "...*And **walk** in love, as Christ also loved us, and gave himself for us an offering and a sacrifice to God for a sweetsmelling savour*" (verse 2). Love is the keynote of the Christian message; God loves us and we are to love one another. Later in chapter 5 we are told: "*For you were sometimes darkness, but now you are light*" (verse 8). "*For the fruit of the light is in all goodness and righteousness and truth*" (verse 9). And then we are exhorted to "*Therefore be careful how you **walk**, not as fools, but as wise*" (verse 15). Walking on the foundation of Ephesians chapters 1, 2 and 3 takes care of this command.

The keyword "Stand" appears four times in chapter 6. "*Put on the whole armor of God, that you may be able to **stand** against the wiles of the devil*" (verse 11). To "stand against the wiles of the devil" is to stand your ground in the face of the enemy's advance. This command is repeated in verse 13, "*Therefore take up the whole armor of God, that you may be able to **stand** in the evil day, and having done all, to **stand**.*" There is no question here of attack on our part; the whole passage speaks of defense, knowing that the victory is already ours. And then we have perhaps the most powerful command of all (verse 14), "***Stand** then...*" or "*Stand therefore...*"

So the structure of Ephesians in itself reveals some vital truths, and contains many God-given concepts that we must think through and apply to our lives accordingly.

Yes, Ephesians, the brightest gem of the epistles to the churches, is the central element in the "curriculum which contains everything necessary for the Christian's standing and his walk." No wonder I'm excited about Ephesians!

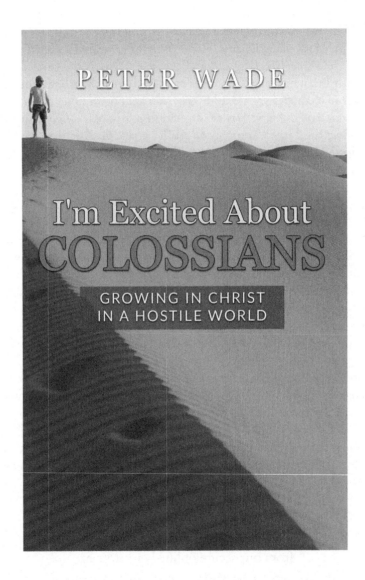

PETER WADE

I'm Excited About
COLOSSIANS

GROWING IN CHRIST
IN A HOSTILE WORLD

Preview

I'm Excited About Colossians

Paul's letter to the Colossians takes us to the heights of revealed truth about Christ perhaps like no other New Testament book. While Ephesians lifts our minds to heavenly places in Christ, Colossians reveals to us Who holds the universe together—Christ Jesus. "The doctrine of the Person of Christ is here stated with greater precision and fulness than in any other of St. Paul's epistles" (Bishop J.B. Lightfoot). This letter should be required reading at least every two or three months, perhaps in different translations each time. It can be read in around 20 minutes but will seed a lifetime of truth and practice.

As I have prepared this work for publication, I have deliberately avoided giving it the look or feel of a commentary. Some may term it a "devotional commentary" but I see it is a journey of inspiration and exploration.

In editing this book for publication, it became obvious that I could not give an attribution for many of my sources. This material was developed as a series while I was a pastor of a local fellowship, and in the busy life of the pastorate I only made sufficient notes to jog my memory when I stood at the podium. I was trained to condense my notes to one page only, preferably no larger than half a letter or A4 page. If I didn't know my subject well enough, then I should not be preaching it!

I searched my memory and my library and can see traces of some headings coming from Warren Wiersbe's book *Be Complete* and accompanying leader's guide with overhead slides, which I have used. I also see Wuest's *Word Studies in the Greek New Testament* on my shelves and *The Church Epistles* by E.W. Bullinger, along with standard reference works. In editing this material I have access on my computer to all the classic reference works and many translations. Since there is nothing new under the sun, I give thanks to those who have gone before and shared their understandings of the Word to all believers.

May you too be "excited about Colossians" and may it become one of your favorite books in God's positive Word.

1

Colossal Colossians!
Colossians 1:1-2

You *can* live and grow in Christ in a hostile world. To live God's way today you need a stable person resident in your life, and that person is Christ. You cannot live a fulfilled life without Christ. I know that there are many books written about positive living that will tell you otherwise, but I believe that so long as you have that empty gap within yourself that only God can fill, you will not live a positive life. Without Him we just *"drifted along on the stream of this world's ideas of living"* (Ephesians 2:2 Phillips). With Him we can do all things. With Him we have fantastic possibilities, and the colossal book of Colossians emphasizes the place of Christ in our lives.

It is interesting to note that Paul never went to Colossae. He did one trip through the area north of the city, but as far as the Bible record is concerned he never visited the city. So he introduces himself as an apostle, since he is writing to a group of people he has never met but about which he has heard much. He is currently under house arrest in Rome, and it is possible he may never get to meet them.

There is an interesting relationship between Ephesus and Colossae; Ephesus is on the coast and Colossae about a hundred miles inland to the east. Acts 19:10 reveals that when Paul stayed at Ephesus for two years, the word of God reached all Asia [Minor], and one of the cities that it reached was Colossae. The believer who actually took the word of God there was a man named Epaphras (Colossians 1:7), who sat at Paul's feet, learned the truth, and then took it home and started what became a powerful and positive church in Colossae, as well as churches in the nearby cities of Laodicea and Hierapolis. All three cities were destroyed by an earthquake around 62 AD.

Ephesians teaches that the believer is in Christ, while Colossians focuses on the Christ that is in the believer. E.W. Bullinger wrote that three-quarters (78) of the 95 verses in Colossians have a marked resemblance to verses in Ephesians (*The Church Epistles*, 2nd ed., 1905, p.175). It is therefore not surprising to see that while "in Christ" in various forms is used 35 times in Ephesians, it is also used 17 times in Colossians, for the truths of "in Christ" and "Christ in" have a vital relationship with each other.

"Paul, an apostle of Christ Jesus by the will of God, and Timothy our brother..." (Colossians 1:1). You may have noticed a difference from the King James and other versions which read "Paul, an apostle of Jesus Christ." The Greek texts use the form "Christ Jesus" in this verse, not "Jesus Christ". What is the difference? Am I any different if I am called Peter Wade or if I am called Wade Peter? Sometimes computer login names have your last name first and then your Christian name or initial, but you are still you. The difference between "Christ Jesus" and "Jesus Christ" is a difference in emphasis. (There are around a dozen different titles given to Christ in the New Testament.)

If Paul was named an apostle of Jesus Christ, the emphasis would be upon the earthly Jesus, the one who was humiliated, the one who was crucified, and who later became the risen, victorious Christ. If Paul was named an apostle of Christ Jesus, then the emphasis is on the risen, victorious Christ who had been humiliated. There is a great difference between those two concepts. Do we worship the the humanity of the Lord, the Jesus of the beard and the sandals? Do we worship the Jesus crucified on the cross? Or do we worship Christ Jesus who sits at the right hand of God in the heavenlies, the powerful, victorious, overcoming one? You have to ask yourself those questions. I worship Christ Jesus, the victorious Son of God. I'm thankful for everything Jesus did for me upon the cross, but I've found in the Bible that God carefully uses words and when He speaks in the revelation to Paul of what He has done for me, it's always the finished work of the victorious Christ Jesus that is in view.

Colossians is written *"to the saints and the faithful brothers in Christ in Colossae ..."* (verse 2a). Not all saints are faithful. A saint in Bible terms is simply a Christian believer. It is not a person who has been canonized by the church years after they have died. A saint is simply a person who believes in God and has accepted Christ as their Savior. There will always be saints, and there will always be faithful brothers and sisters.

Made in the USA
Columbia, SC
13 January 2021